ABOUT THE BOOK

The theory of evolution may be generally
accepted, but how is it proved? In this
first definitive, easy-to-follow guide to
the subject, Mr Lehman brings together the
bare bones of evolution.
A fascinating combination of detective work
and rigorous scientific enquiry, *The Proofs
of Evolution* fills a long-standing gap in
scientific literature for the layman.

GOOD
READ

ABOUT THE AUTHOR

J. P. Lehman is professor at the
Museum of Natural History in Paris.

THE PROOFS OF EVOLUTION

J. P. Lehman

Translated by Patricia Crampton

GORDON & CREMONESI

© Presses Universitaires de France 1973
© Translation Gordon Cremonesi Ltd 1977

First published as *Les Preuves Paléontologiques
de L'Evolution* by Presses Universitaires de France 1973

This edition published with corrections and additions 1977

Design by Heather Gordon

Text set in 11/12 pt. Photon Baskerville,
printed by photolithography, and bound in
Great Britain at The Pitman Press, Bath

British Library/Library of Congress
Cataloguing in Publication Data

Lehman, J. P.
    The Proofs of Evolution
    1. Evolution
    I. Title II. Crampton, Patricia
    575   QH366.2   77-30170

ISBN 0-86033-055-9

Gordon & Cremonesi Publishers
London and New York
New River House
34 Seymour Road
London N8 0BE

Contents

GEOLOGICAL TIME SCALE

era	period	epoch	duration (millions of years)	no. of years ago (millions)
Cenozoic	Quaternary	Holocene	10,000 yrs. app.	
		Pleistocene	2.5	
				— 2.5 —
	Tertiary	Pliocene	4.5	
				— 7 —
		Miocene	19	
				— 26 —
		Oligocene	12	
				— 38 —
		Eocene	16	
				— 54 —
		Palaeocene	11	
				— 65 —
Mesozoic	Cretaceous		71	
				— 136 —
	Jurassic		54	
				— 190 —
	Triassic		35	
				— 225 —
Palaeozoic	Permian		55	
				— 280 —
	Carboniferous Pennsylvanian		45	
				— 325 —
	Carboniferous Mississippian		20	
				— 345 —
	Devonian		50	
				— 395 —
	Silurian		35	
				— 430 —
	Ordovician		70	
				— 500 —
	Cambrian		70	
				— 570 —
	Precambrian		4,000	

Introduction

According to the theory of evolution, organisms descended from one another, changing as they went. More than a century and a half after Lamarck (*La Philosophie Zoologique*, 1809), and more than a century after Darwin (whose *Origin Of Species* appeared in 1859), this idea can now no longer be regarded as a hypothesis. The scientific progress of the nineteenth and twentieth centuries—in palaeontology in particular—has provided ample proof of the evolution of life. Nevertheless the public obviously accepts transformism with some reservations, for reasons which are difficult to analyse. Given the attitude of the Church to this subject, these doubts do not appear to have a religious basis these days. More probably, they are simply a mixture of traditional prejudices and ignorance.

The theory of evolution took a long time to make headway, because it was first necessary to know how to interpret fossils; at first they were regarded as freaks of nature or as the remains of very recent, more or less historical organisms. Fossils have certainly always fascinated man; for instance, fossil molluscs were used as jewellery in prehistoric times and in ancient times Strabo reported that fossil sea-shells had been found in areas far removed from the sea. But observations of this kind seem to have been rather exceptional; for instance, although Pliny had seen fossils he thought they were connected with thunderbolts or were simply freaks of nature. Empedocles described fossil hippopotamus bones from Sicily as the bones of giants, an interpretation which lasted for a long time, since even under Louis XIV there were debates about fossil elephant bones, which some people still took to be giants' bones. The descriptions of such bones were assembled in "gigantologies"; fragments of bones of proboscideans—which can be seen in the Gallery of Palaeontology of the Natural History Museum—were actually classified as the skeleton of the giant Teutobocchus, King of the Cimbri, Marius' enemy, according to the legend. Yet Avicenna, the great eleventh century Arab philosopher, and Albert the Great in the thirteenth century, had already accepted the living origins of fossils.

However, the clearest conclusions on fossils were expressed by Leonardo da Vinci and Bernard Palissy in the sixteenth century. Leonardo da Vinci, with his understanding of the principle of actual causes, according to which geological phenomena have been determined by constant factors throughout the history of the Earth, did not accept that fossils could have formed on mountain tops under the influence of the stars, since nothing of the kind existed in his day. And Bernard Palissy opened a Natural Science Exhibition in 1575 in Paris where he exhibited numerous fossils. "A potter who knew neither Latin nor Greek was the first person who dared to say in Paris towards the end of the sixteenth century, and in the face of all the scholars, that fossil shells were real shells deposited in the past by the sea ..." (Fontenelle). Nor, in defiance of many contemporary naturalists, did Palissy accept that fossils were the vestiges of the Great Flood. Nicolas Steno, the Danish scholar who lived in Florence, showed in 1667 that the petrified objects known as glossopetra (or "stone tongues"—that is of birds or snakes) were the teeth of sharks; this view had already been proposed by the Italian Fabius Columna, but Steno stuck to his diluvian explanations. In the eighteenth century, fossils were almost unanimously acknowledged to be the remnants of organisms, but it was still often thought that they were the remains of flood victims: e.g.

the famous *Homo diluvii testis* (FIG. 1), the man bearing witness to the flood, described in 1726 by Scheuchzer, which was simply a Japanese salamander of the Swiss Upper Tertiary. Under these conditions Voltaire's scepticism with regard to fossils seemed downright old-fashioned for his time. "Petrified fish",

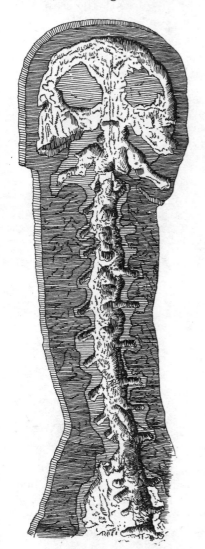

FIG. 1.—*Andrias scheuchzeri* after the engraving published in 1755 in Dargenville's *Oryctologie*. This Japanese salamander from the Swiss Upper Tertiary was thought by Scheuchzer, the first author to describe it, in the 18th century, to be the remnants of a man drowned in the Flood, *Homo diluvii testis*.

he wrote, "are simply rare fish rejected by Romans at table because they were not fresh" (Voltaire, 1746).

Of course, it was fundamental to the development of palaeontology to understand the living origin of fossils, but there was another new idea which had yet to be accepted. This was the observation that some of the fossils were the remnants of organisms which have completely vanished today.

It was Buffon who observed that many ancient species are now extinct. In particular, he looked at some unknown teeth (FIG. 2) brought back from Ohio by a French officer. These

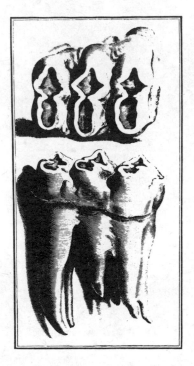

FIG. 2.—The first mastodon tooth, described by Buffon.

huge teeth had rows of cusps and no comparable teeth are known in living nature. Buffon attributed them to a vanished animal (which Cuvier named the Mastodon). He also believed these Mastodons to be much bigger than they really were, because he thought that there were more than one molar per half-jaw in the mouth (this American mastodon is often wrongly referred to as a mammoth).

It was left to Cuvier to prove that vanished species were quite a frequent phenomenon. Cuvier is undeniably the father of modern palaeontology; it was Cuvier who showed how fossils should be studied, that is, in the light of comparative anatomy. He gave a masterly exposition in his *Recherches sur les Ossemens fossiles* (1812) of how he had worked out the skeletal structure of the two principal ungulates (FIG. 3) from the Montmartre gypsum beds, the odd-toed (Perissodactyl) *Palaeontherium* and the even-toed (Artiodactyl) *Anoplotherium*. Presented with a few isolated bones, he was able to assemble them according to their affinities "in obedience to comparative anatomy, every bone, every fragment of bone, took up its rightful place." When complete skeletons of these animals were afterwards finally found, they confirmed Cuvier's conclusions. Cuvier knew all the fossil vertebrate finds made in his day. He was the first to describe and research systematically the mammals of the Montmartre gypsum. The descriptive value of his work was so sound that no one has ventured to revive the study of his material.

Then how can we explain Cuvier's dogmatism, apparently so much in contrast to his palaeontological observations? We know that Cuvier believed that the earth had been inhabited by successive faunas which had disappeared but he believed that each of these fauna was the result of successive divine creations. One of his claims was that men and monkeys had appeared in the last creation and that consequently there could be neither fossil men nor fossil monkeys differing from the living ones. The only way to understand Cuvier's views on evolution is to place oneself in the atmosphere of the day. At the beginning of the nineteenth century scholars had no idea of the length of geological time. The Book of Genesis implies a relatively brief geological time-scale of 6,000 years. Although it is probable that Cuvier, following Buffon, did not accept this figure, it is certain that he would not have been able to conceive the 600 million years which modern scientists attribute merely to the eras during which sedimentary formations have contained fossils (from the Cambrian to the present). When Cuvier describes the anatomy of a mummified ibis from Egypt with great conscientiousness and can see no difference between the ibis of the ancient Egyptians and the modern ibis, we can see that he is wrong to conclude that evolution never happened, because ancient Egypt is very close to modern times and evolution obviously cannot be observed over a period which is geologically short—but which seemed very long to Cuvier.

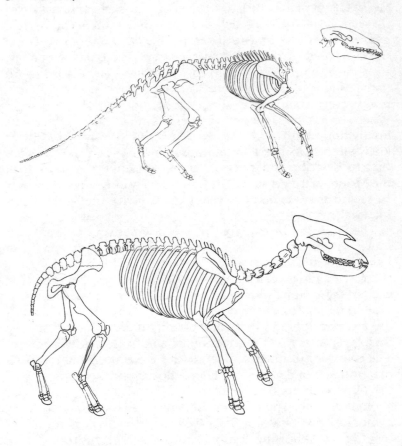

FIG. 3.—Reconstructions of (**A**) *Anoplotherium* and (**B**) *Palaeotherium*, according to Cuvier.

On the other hand, Cuvier tried to stick closely to the facts, rejecting unverified hypotheses. Many eighteenth and nineteenth century authors had proposed transformist systems which were quite unacceptable. We have only to remember the claims of De Maillet, who under the pseudonym Telliamed published the *Nouveau système du monde, ou entretien de Telliamed, philosophe indien, avec un missionaire français.* According to De Maillet, for instance, the fish were the ancestors of the birds; after being trapped in clumps of reeds, the gills of some fish were supposed to have turned into wings. Similarly, the ideas of Étienne Geoffroy Saint-Hilaire on the common design of insects ("dermo-vertebrates" with "external vertebrae", as this author put it) and vertebrates (Geoffroy's "high vertebrates") were simply baseless fantasies. One can imagine Cuvier's opposition to theories like these. Nevertheless, somewhat paradoxically it was Cuvier who was responsible for the development of vertebrate palaeontology, the science which has provided the clearest proofs of evolution.

Almost throughout the 19th century, however, palaeontologists such as Agassiz, von Meyer and Owen were content to describe new fossil forms. It is rather odd that to prove the evolution of species Darwin based his arguments mainly on anatomy, embryology, and bio-geography. All the same, he had observed that the fauna of the Tertiary mammals of South America was quite different from that of his day, although the same groups of animals were found (edentates and marsupials).

It was the work of Thomas Huxley in England, Gaudry in France, author of the first French treatise on evolutionary palaeontology, the *Enchaînements du monde animal,* and the Americans Cope and Marsh, which showed that evolution generally brought about increasing complexity (example: specialisation of limbs and dentition, development of the brain in mammals). In 1882 Thomas Huxley was formulating the problems perfectly, and his conclusions are still completely valid:

The well-established truths of palaeontology . . . at the present time have left room for only two hypotheses. The first is

summed up as follows: in the course of Earth's history in-
numerable species of animals and plants have come into
being independently of one another an incalculable number
of times. This theory therefore implies either spontaneous
generation of an astonishing kind ... or belief in an incalculable number of creations over periods whose length
cannot be calculated. The other hypothesis would have it
that the species of animals and plants have followed each
other, the last proceeding from the gradual modification of
the first. This is the theory of evolution: the palaeontological
discoveries of the last ten years are so much in agreement
with this hypothesis that if it did not exist, palaeontology
would have to invent it.

CHAPTER ONE

The First Organisms

Palaeontology teaches us that various organisms have appeared successively on the surface of the earth and that many forms have disappeared altogether. It also shows us that the first groups of plants and animals were still relatively simple and that life has evolved towards greater complexity.

Basically, the fossil-bearing epochs began with the Cambrian period near the beginning of the Palaeozoic, some 600 million years ago. A few fossil organisms and evidence of living activity have, in fact, been found before the Cambrian, in the Precambrian era. In 1914 the American palaeontologist Walcott discovered and described special formations, stromatoliths, which he believed to be algae in the Montana Precambrian (Belt series). These formations did have a structure indicating some degree of organisation: laminated in the stromatolith described by Walcott under the name of *Collenia*, with concentric bands connected by radial walls in *Newlandia* (FIG. 4), and with irregular juxtaposed, cylindical or pentagonal tubes in *Greysonia*. Since then a variety of stromatoliths has been found in much more recent terrains (Permotriassic, for instance, about 250 million years ago). These formations do not seem to be at all unique to the Precambrian. They are

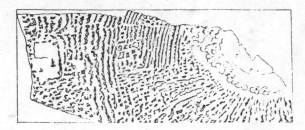

FIG. 4.—A stromatolith: *Newlandia* (cross-section). (*According to Walcott*)

no longer interpreted along Walcott's lines. Although certain stromatoliths are of purely mineral origin (*Greysonia*) they seem to have resulted much more frequently from the precipitation of limestone on filaments of Cyanophyta (blue algae) impregnated with mucus. In fact, no algae structure has ever been observed in stromatoliths, having completely vanished. However, some large fossil stromatoliths (some are more than 7 m long) may be the remnants of reefs of Cyanophyta. In any case, the existence of the stromatoliths does seem to show that the Cyanophyta are among the first plants to have appeared on the surface of the earth: small stromatoliths (oncoliths) from the area near Bulawayo in Rhodesia have been found in crystalline rock some 2,500 million years old.

The existence of fossil bacteria is still highly controversial. For instance, the name *Eobacterium isolatum* has recently been given to the small fossil rods seen under the electronic microscope in fragments of silica dissolved in hydrofluoric acid from a Precambrian formation in Swaziland (Transvaal). This dates from about 3,000 million years ago. But there is nothing to prove that these supposed bacteria are really the remains of organisms. Since the bacteria are considered to be relatively close to the Cyanophyta, it is probable that they did exist in the Precambrian. This is indirectly proved by the existence in the Precambrian of ferruginous and phosphate rocks, some of which should be of bacterial origin.

The Ontario Precambrian flints described by Barghoorn and Tyler are particularly rich in fossil plants; these are about 2,000 million years old. The organisms in these flints were observed on thin slides (more than 800 slides were prepared) or detached by maceration in hydrofluoric acid. Barghoorn and Tyler picked out septated organisms with elongated (*Gunflintia*) or short (*Animikia*) cells; these fossils are probably related to the present-day Cyanophyta *Oscillatoria*. Other filamentous organisms contain corpuscles which are sporiform (*Entosphaerites*) or more often ramified (*Archaeorestis*) or sometimes arranged radially (*Eoastrion*), but most of the 'genera' studied by Barghoorn and Tyler are not readily open to interpretation. Nevertheless, these observations lead to the conclusion that plant life did begin on earth with quite simple organisms, and mainly with the cyanophytes.

As far as animal life is concerned, very few Precambrian fossils have been discovered and finds have in most cases been isolated. For instance, a trace of Arenicola was found in the Precambrian north of Lake Hudson (*Rhizonetron*), and there are a Precambrian Medusa from Arizona, and some pennatulidae (coelenterata related to the present-day Alcyonaria, in South-West Africa and Great Britain). On the other hand, the Montana brachiopod (Belt series, *Linguella,* FIG. 5) originally

FIG. 5.—One of the oldest known Brachiopods: *Linguella* from the Cambrian of Montana. (*After Fenton*)

attributed to the Precambrian, seems to be merely Cambrian.

Other examples could be quoted, but it is important to emphasise that the identification of Precambrian organisms is often highly controversial both as to the biological nature of the fossils and as to their Precambrian age.

It is the Ediacara fauna which supplies the most distinct and complete information on life in the Precambrian era. This deposit was discovered in 1947 and lies about 300 km north of Adelaide. The fossils are so numerous that the site has been

turned into a fossil reserve, protected by the Australian
Government. The first authors regarded this deposit as Lower
Cambrian, but recently Glaessner has shown that the Ediacara
quartzite which produced the fossils was well below the Lower
Cambrian: it was therefore Precambrian, but of a late stage.
The Ediacara fauna (FIG. 6) is quite varied and specimens are

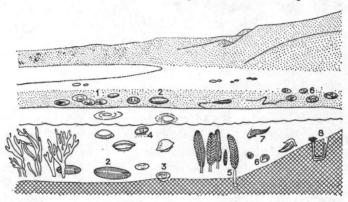

FIG. 6.—Reconstruction of Ediacara shoreline and fauna. 1. Hypothetical algae
and sponges (not yet found in the deposit); 2. Segmented worm (*Dickinsonia*); 3.
Tribrachidium (unexplained organism which may have been an echinoderm); 4.
Medusae; 5. *Rangea* and *Charnia* (Coelentera related to living pennatulids); 6.
Parvancorina, unexplained organism; 7. Segmented worm (*Spriggina*); 8.
Segmented worm in tubular habitat (*after Glaessner*).

numerous (about 1,000 have been collected). This fauna comprises Coelentarata (more than six genera of jelly-fish, divided
into various groups), pennatulids, or sea-pens (*Rangea* and
Pteridinium), segmented worms (*Spriggina, Dickinsonia*) and unexplained organisms, with perhaps one echinoderm
(*Tribrachidium*). None of these organisms of the Ediacara fauna
has a shell, whereas shelled invertebrates do appear—at
Ediacara too—in higher (i.e., more recent) strata. Metabolism
of the limestone, enabling a skeleton or shell to be built, would
not yet seem to have been acquired in the Precambrian and
probably did not appear until the Lower Cambrian. But
whether this hypothesis is true or false, it must be observed that
at present the Precambrian has revealed no molluscs, no

echinoderms—with the exception of *Tribrachidium*, if it is an echinoderm—and no arthropods or vertebrates. Thus the evidence of the first fossils is precisely in agreement with the idea that evolution has brought about increasing diversification and specialisation in living creatures.

CHAPTER TWO

The Evolution of the Plant Kingdom

As we have just seen, bacteria and Cyanophyta already existed in the Precambrian era. Among the thallophytes, green algae have been found dating from the Cambrian (the Dasycladaceae family, in particular—algae with non-septated axis and

FIG. 7.—Solenopore (red algae) cross-section (× 30 app.). (*After Mme Maslova*)

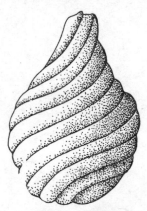

FIG. 8.—One of the first known "fructifications" of fossil Charophyta: *Trochiliscus* (× 70 app). (*After Croft*)

whorled branches—began in the Siberian Cambrian). Red algae have also existed since the Cambrian, with the solenopores (FIG. 7) whose structure is similar to that of the present day *Lithothamnium*. Of the brown algae, the diatoms also appear in the Cambrian (Siberia; this seems to be a family related to the diatoms, rather than diatoms proper). The other (non-monocellular) brown algae appeared later, but this is not surprising because their remains are rarely found, since they fossilise so badly.

Fossil fungi are in general difficult to detect. The oldest are Devonian and seem to resemble the present-day *Saprolegnia* (which develop on the bodies of insects and dead fish).

Charophyta have been found, thanks to isolated "fructifications" (e.g. *Trochiliscus*) in the Lower Devonian (FIG. 8).

Other non-vascular cryptogams include Bryophyta in the Polish Ordovician (*Musciphyton, Hepaticaephyton*) and *Sporognites* in the Australian Upper Silurian, but it is quite possible that isolated bryophyte spores existed before the Ordovician. Various authors have described spores—often tetrahedral and cutinised—in Cambrian areas (Gotland, Estonia, Kashmir). It is always very difficult to be certain that such tiny fossils are in their right place or have been carried into the formation from elsewhere.

Did vascular plants already exist in the Cambrian? The problem is certainly debatable. Fragments of tracheids accompanying spores have been described in the Indian Cambrian. In the Siberian Cambrian, axes almost ten centimetres in length have been observed which certainly seem to possess a vascular structure (*Aldanophyton*) and have been regarded as the remains of lycopodiineae, but this interpretation is controversial. On the other hand, even if there were a few, very rare vascular cryptogams in the Cambrian, the general picture would not be altered, since these plants must have been present in very small numbers.

It is in the Upper Silurian that we see the first vascular cryptogams appearing. These are psilophyta of the *Cooksonia* and *Haliserites* genera (FIGS. 9A and B). In the lowest Devonian period, only the psilophytes have been confirmed with certain-

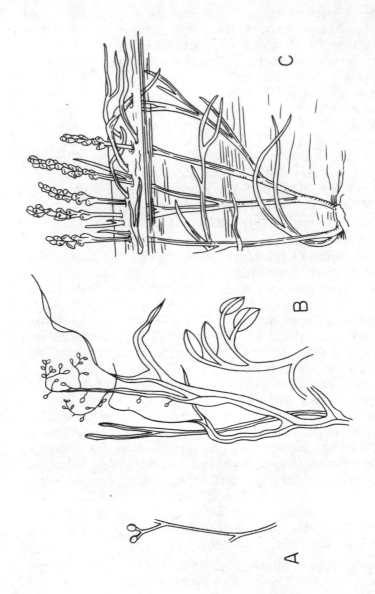

FIG. 9.—Various Psilophytala: **A**, *Cooksonia*; **B**, *Haliserites*; **C**, *Zosterophyllum* (**A**, *after Andrews*; **B**, *after Emberger*; **C**, *after Kräusel and Wieland*)

ty (*Cooksonia, Zosterophyllum*). (FIG. 9C). At the top of the Lower
Devonian (Coblenzian), psilophytes are still present, but the
lycophytes are beginning to appear (*Baragwanathia* a genus
formerly wrongly regarded as Upper Silurian) (FIG. 10). The
first pteridospermea (ovular fern), structurally comparable to a
seed, but in which the embryo does not feed at the expense of

FIG. 10.—The first known lycophyte, *Baragwanathia*. (*After Lang
and Cookson*)

FIG. 11.–Forked tips of a frond
of the first known
Pteridospermea: *Aneurophyton*.
(*After Banks*).

the mother as in the phanerogam, appears in the Eifelian (bottom of the Middle Devonian). This is the *Aneurophyton* family
(FIG. 11). From the top of the Middle Devonian (Givetian) we
know of true ferns, pteridospermeae and articulata (present-
day horse-tail group, genus *Hyenia*, FIG. 12).

The stratigraphic distribution is of some importance, since
from the anatomical point of view the psilophyta do seem to be
the oldest vascular cryptogams. Owing to the simplicity of their
structure, particularly clear in the *Rhynia* genus (FIG. 13B) of the
Scottish Middle Devonian, most palaeo-botanists have
regarded the psilophyta as the ancestors of vascular plants, an
opinion supported by Hirmer, Seward and Zimmerman. The
psilophytes take their name, of course, from the *Psilophyton*

family (FIG. 13A) from the Lower Devonian of Gaspé (Canada) described in 1859; this plant reaches a maximum height of one

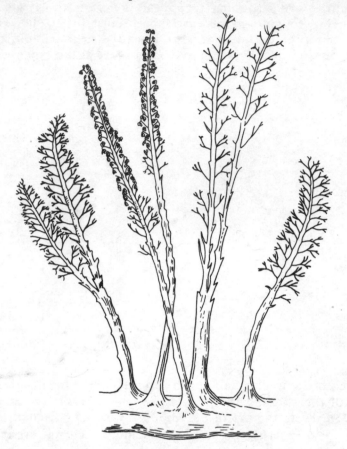

FIG. 12.—One of the first Articulata, genus *Hyeniae* (× 0.9). (*After Kräusel and Wieland*)

metre; it has a spiny axis, branching, but with irregular branches, rising from quite a large rhizome. Also included among the psilophytes are the *Rhynia, Horneophyton, Cooksonia* and *Zosterophyllum* families.

The vegetative equipment of *Rhynia* was a vascularised

dichotomised thallus, having a central vascular bundle with bast and tracheids under a parenchymatous cortex. The upper end of the thallus consisted of spore cases with spores grouped in tetrads. *Horneophyton* differs from *Rhynia* by possessing a central pouch of sterile tissue in the spore case. In *Cooksonia* the spore cases are ovoid as distinct from the fusiform ones of the two preceding families.

Zosterophyllum, from the German Lower Devonian, had lateral spore cases grouped in a kind of spike. Also classed among the psilophytes was *Asteroxylon* (FIG. 13C) of the Rhynie Devonian; this plant was covered with small, close-set leaves, with pear-shaped spore cases and a xylem with a star-shaped cross section.

This classical idea that the psilophytes were archaic was criticised by Axelrod in 1959. In his view the psilophytes, obviously heterogeneous (their appearance, for instance, does differ greatly) had appeared at the same time as the lycophytes (as was then believed) and their structural simplicity should be regarded as the result of a regression.

These viewpoints were not generally accepted, especially by Banks (1968). In his study he showed that the chronological succession of the first vascular cryptogams is completely in conformity with the principle of the increasing complexity of organisms during the Upper Silurian and Devonian periods. Banks also excluded the *Psilophyton* and *Asteroxylon* genera from the psilophytes and this new restricted definition of psilophytes makes them homogeneous; they contain two big groups:
1. the RHYNIOPHYTINA, with terminal spore cases and bare stems (*Rhynia, Horneophyton, Cooksonia*, etc.); 2. the ZOSTEROPHYLLITINA, with lateral spore cases (Zosterophyllum etc.). In this subdivision Banks sees a major dichotomy in the history of the plant kingdom (diphyletism). The lycophytes would then be descended from the Zosterophyllitina via *Asteroxylon*, which is already a lycophyte (the star-shaped xylem found in *Asteroxylon* is reproduced in *Colpodexylon*, another lycophyte of the Middle and Upper Devonian), whereas the ferns and pteridospermeae would be descended from the Rhyniaeceae (*Psilophyton* representing an intermediate stage in the transformation). Whatever one may

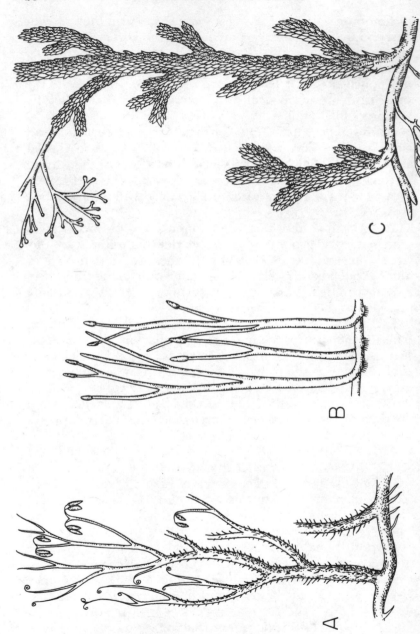

FIG. 13.—Other Psilophytala. **A,** *Philophyton* (× 1/6 app.); **B,** *Rhynia* (× 1/3 app.); **C,** *Asteroxylon* (× 1/2 app.). (**A,** *after Fenton*; **B,**

think of this diphyletic hypothesis, we can conclude that the clearly primitive anatomical structure of the psilophytes is in absolute agreement with their great geological antiquity.

Moreover we have seen that in the Devonian the organisation of the main plant groups, apart from seed plants, has already been elaborated. These blue-prints cover groups which are now quite unimportant or not very diversified in living nature (lycopods, horse-tails, ferns), but before regressing they were to flourish in the Carboniferous (FIG. 14), giving rise to the main constituents of the coal forest. Apart from the psilophytes, the coal forest comprised: 1. Lycophytes, with trees such as the Lepidodendria, Sigillaria, Bothrodendracea etc.; 2. Articulata—of which the horse-tails are the sole living representatives—with the Sphenophyllala and the Calamites;

FIG. 14.—Reconstruction of carboniferous forest. 1, *Sphenopteris*; 2, *Odontopteris*; 3, *Neuropteris*; 4, *Lepidodendron*; 5, *Sigillaria*; 6, *Calamites*; 7, *Cordaites*; 8, *Mariopteris*; 9, Tree-ferns. (*After P. Bertrand*)

3. Arborescent ferns; 4. Pteridospermeae and related plants, the Cordaitalae; 5. Conifers (*Lebachia* appeared in the Middle Carboniferous).

The advent of seed in the higher plants should not be thought of as a sudden new "invention" of nature, but as a process affecting various trends. For instance, in the lycophyte *Cystoporites* (a megaspore of *Lepidocarpon*), there is a single ovule represented by the megaspore (FIG. 15), the other three spores having aborted.

In some *Lepidocarpon*, moreover, this megaspore, as it developed, seems to have given birth to a true plantula under the still intact wall of the spore. In the pteridospermeae, as we have said, there was still no seed, properly speaking (Mangenot), because, whereas in the phanerogam the embryo in the seed grows on the actual mother feeding it (viviparous), the ovule of the pteridospermeae is independent of the mother

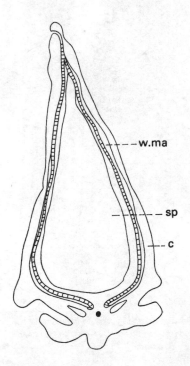

FIG. 15.—Cross-section of a macrospore of *Lepidocarpon*. (*After Scott*) **w.ma.** wall of macrosporangium; **sp,** macrospore; **c,** seed coat

(oviparous). But the ovule of the pteridospermeae is covered by differentiated teguments resembling seed coats.

The lesson of palaeontology is that the evolution of the plant kingdom tended towards the appearance of the flower and the seed. The gymnosperms were followed by the angiosperms. In the Jurassic and Lower Cretaceous the gymnosperms clearly predominated. It was at this point that the Bennettitina reached their apogee. It is accepted that the angiosperms were taking over from the gymnosperms from the Upper Cretaceous onwards, but they probably appeared much earlier. Leaves resembling palm fronds have been described in the Californian Middle Triassic (*Sanmiguelia*) (FIG. 16), and leaves recalling those of the willow in the Lower Lias of Greenland (*Furcula*)

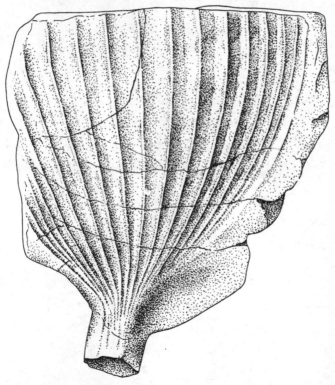

FIG. 16.—The first known angiosperm leaf: *Sanmiguelia* (× 1/3). (*After Brown*)

(FIG. 17). These discoveries and other comparable ones do not alter the fundamental conclusion, however, that the angiosperms are later than the gymnosperms and their expansion dates from the Upper Cretaceous.

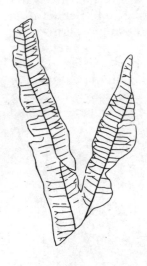

FIG. 17.—One of the first known Angiosperms: *Furcula* (× 0.9). (*After Harris*)

From this brief and incomplete analysis we can therefore conclude that the history of the plant kingdom is explicable only in the light of evolution.

CHAPTER THREE

The Evolution of Invertebrates

As we saw above in relation to the first fossils, most of the invertebrate classes are unknown in the Precambrian. A great deal of invertebrate history is missing because the Precambrian fossils were widely destroyed during the transformation of sedimentary rocks into crystalline rocks (metamorphism). We know that the annelids, bryozoans, brachiopods, molluscs, arthropods and echinoderms already existed in the Cambrian. All the great classes of invertebrates had appeared. Evolution can only be demonstrated *within* the invertebrate classes, however, between successive orders or families, rather than at the level of the origin of these classes.

We will take just a few examples to show that the various classes of invertebrates have been subject to evolution. There are of course some genera which have not changed at all in geological time: for instance, the lingula. No arguments against evolution can be drawn from this, because, on the one hand, such examples are exceptional, and, on the other hand, the appearance of the lingula—the brachiopods were already a highly evolved group—could only have been the outcome of a long previous history, although one about which there is no evidence.

I. Cnidaria (Coelenterata)

Without going into the very complex details of coelenterate evolution, we can simply recall their dominant characteristics. Coelenterates existed in the Precambrian, as we have seen. In the Palaeocene, three large groups of coelenterate reef-makers, which subsequently disappeared in the Ordovician, play a fundamental role: the tetracorals, the tabulates and the

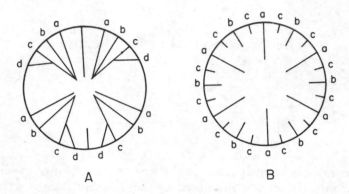

A   B

FIG. 18.—Diagrammatic cross-sections of the calyx of A tetracorals (in which the chambers appear in fours or cycles of four); and B hexacorals (in which the chambers appear in sixes or multiples of six). The letters designate chambers of the same cycle. (*After Shrock and Twenhofel*)

stromatopores. In the tetracorals, the septa of the skeleton of each individual in the colony are arranged in cycles of four (FIG. 18A). In the tabulates the basic skeleton of each individual chamber is occupied by transverse sub-parallel septa which are generally reduced to the form of tubercles or spines. The stromatospores have a skeleton of concentric calcareous strata joined by irregular vertical columns. All these groups disappear just before the Triassic. In the Mesozoic, the true hexacorals (FIG. 18B)—which include the madrepores—appear but do not form reefs until the Jurassic; these Jurassic hexacorals are quite different from the modern genera, in contrast to the Cretaceous hexacorals, which are much more similar to the modern forms.

II. Bryozoans

These colonising animals comprise tiny individuals, or zoids, each living in a calcareous or membranous chamber, the zoaria. The outstanding feature of bryozoan evolution is the increasing complexity of the zoaria. The most recent group, the cheilostomata, which appeared at the beginning of the Cretaceous, have zoaria closed by a hinged lid.

III. Brachiopods

Brachiopods were still unknown in the Precambrian (see CHAPTER ONE). By the time of the Cambrian they were numerous. Although there was a very high proportion of Inarticulata (e.g. lingula), some Articulata (Orthis) already existed and included a family, the Palaeotremata (genus *Rustella*) without stem, which was exclusively Cambrian. By the time of the Ordovician, the proportion of articulates was greater and most of the families of articulates had come into being. The Upper Silurian was distinguished by the dominance of one family, the Pentameracea, which was to be mainly replaced in the Devonian by the Spiriferacea. At the beginning of the Mesozoic, only a few relics of Inarticulata survived. Almost all the articulate families have disappeared, apart from those of the Rhynchonellida, Terebratulida and Terebratella, which survive today.

IV. Molluscs

Gastropods have existed since the Lower Cambrian. Diotocards (with two little ears and two kidneys) appeared in the Upper Cambrian, reaching their apogee during the Palaeozoic and then regressing, although they are still numerous today. The Monotocards (with one earlet and one kidney) appeared in the Silurian but were rare in the Palaeozoic. The Pulmonata seem to have existed since the Carboniferous but only developed in quantity in the Jurassic.

As far as the lamellibranchia are concerned, new families became distinct principally in the Triassic. The Jurassic and Cretaceous periods saw the differentiation of the reef-making lamellibranchia—the Rudists—which disappeared at the end of the Mesozoic.

Among the cephalopods the evolution of the Belemnites is marked by variations in the length of the ventral cone. Among the sepioidea there was a series of forms (*Beloptera, Belosepia*), in which the guard regressed (FIG. 19). In the cuttle-bone the guard was greatly reduced, but this transformation does not mean that the *Beloptera, Belosepia* and *Sepia* belong to the same line. The nautiloids appeared in the Lower Cambrian, evolving mainly in the Ordovician. At this stage the straight nautiloid shells (orthocones) began to coil, giving rise to other genera (FIG. 20); the orthocones regress in the Carboniferous and Permian in favour of these coiled forms.

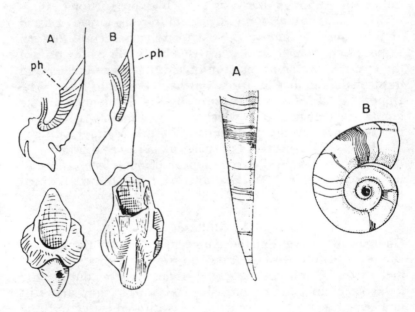

FIG. 19.—Two skeletons of evolved cephalopods: (**A**) *Beloptera* and (**B**) *Belosepia*; **ph**, phragmocone (part of skeleton corresponding to ammonite chambers). (*After Roger*)

FIG. 20.—Progressive coiling of the Nautila. (**A**) *Rhynchothoceras*; (**B**) *Cyclolituites*. (*After Schindewolf*)

The first ammonoids were the Devonian Goniatites and Clymenia with a relatively simple suture (line on the shell defining the separation of two consecutive chambers). In the Triassic, ammonites with a suture line predominate; they bear deeply incised concave parts towards the front (lobes) only (Ceratites). Generally speaking, the suture line of Jurassic and Cretacean ammonites is still more divided, although there are exceptions (FIG. 21).

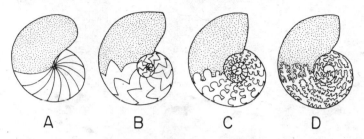

A   B   C   D

FIG. 21.—Form of the septa in (A) **Nautilus,** (B) a Goniatite, (C) a Ceratite and (D) an Ammonite. (*After Boule and Piveteau*)

V. Arthropods

As an example, we will simply recall the broad outlines of insect evolution. The insects made their first appearance with the genus *Rhyneilla* (FIG. 22) which was a collembola. In the

FIG. 22.—The first known insect: *Rhyniella (after Scourfield)*

Carboniferous, the insect fauna, apart from Blattaria and Homoptera (the group to which the present-day grasshopper belongs), comprised only groups which have now disappeared: Palaeodictyoptera, e.g. *Stenodictya*. (FIG. 23); Protodonata, some

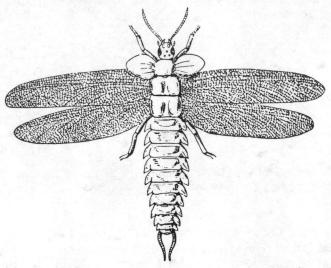

FIG. 23.—A carboniferous insect, the Palaeodictyoptera, Stenodictya (× 1/2 app.). (*After Handlirsch*)

reminiscent of the present-day butterfly; Protorthoptera; Protoephemeroida. The appearance of the insects which underwent complete metamorphosis dates from the Permian (Holometabola), including the Coleoptera, in particular. The first known Diptera and Hymenoptera date from the Jurassic. The Lepidoptera appear to be much more recent: they have so far been detected only from the Eocene onwards; their development is probably linked with that of the flowering plants. So we see that all in all the Hemimetabola (incomplete metamorphosis) are older than the Holometabola and that the orders commonly considered the most highly evolved (Diptera, Hymenoptera, Lepidoptera), are fairly recent.

VI. Echinoderms

Of the *Echinodermata* we know of fixed forms only (Pelmatozoa) in the Cambrian, some of them flat and bilaterally symmetrical (Carpoids) (FIG. 24), but the Crinoids proper (the modern

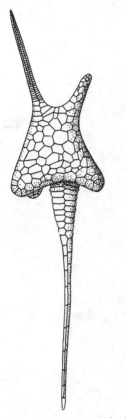

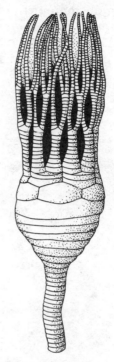

FIG. 25.—A crinoid from the Jurassic: *Apiocrinus* (× 2/3 app.). (*After Cuénot*)

FIG. 24.—A carpoid from the Ordovician (Lower Palaeozoic): *Dendrocystis* (× 2/3 app.). (*After Bather*)

representative of this group is the Comatula) did not appear until the Ordovician. The primary groups of Crinoids disappeared in the Permian and Triassic and were replaced in the

Triassic by a group with particularly mobile arms, the Articulata (FIG. 25).

Of the free echinoderms (Eleutherozoa), the Echinoids started in the Palaeozoic with forms related to the Palaechinoids as a whole (this is not a natural group), in which there were generally more than two series of plates per interambulacrum and often the same per ambulacrum (e.g. *Melonechinus*) (FIG. 26). The genus *Eothuria* (FIG. 27) from the Upper Ordovician, often classed with the Palaechinoids, seems close to the origins of the Holothuria.

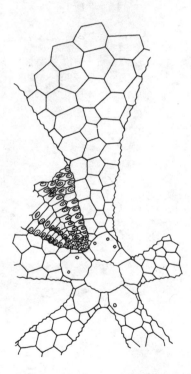

FIG. 26.—Upper pole of skeleton of a Palaechinoid urchin, *Melonechinus*. Note the ambulacra with more than two series of plates. (*After Jackson*)

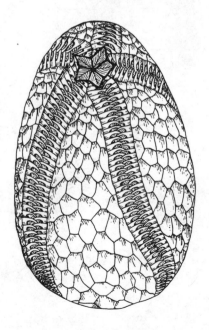

FIG. 27.—*Eothuria* (× 1 app.). (*After Macbride and Spencer*)

In the Permian, the Palaechinoids disappeared and were replaced by the regular or endocyclic urchins (with radial symmetry) (FIG. 28). They were characterised by ambulacra and interambulacra with two series of plates each. The irregular urchins (FIG. 29) or exocyclics, with bilateral symmetry, (like the modern Spatangus) appeared in the Jurassic and survived alongside the regular urchins. In the exocyclics, the anus migrates along the animal's plane of symmetry and the mouth often migrates in the opposite direction.

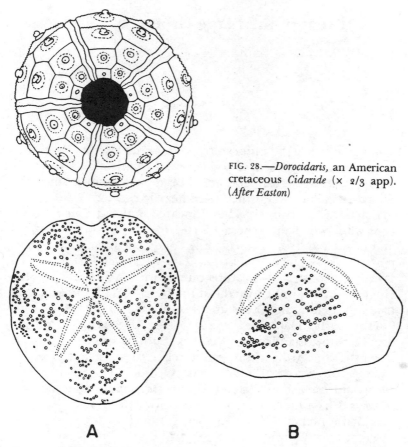

FIG. 28.—*Dorocidaris,* an American cretaceous *Cidaride* (× 2/3 app). (*After Easton*)

A   **B**

FIG. 29.—A living Spatangus: **A** skeleton viewed from above and **B** from the side.

CHAPTER FOUR

The Advent of the Large Groups of Vertebrates

The Agnatha are the oldest fossil vertebrates known. Devoid of jaws, they are represented today by soft, jawless forms such as lampreys and hagfish and have been in existence since the Siluro-Devonian when they were heavily ossified (Osteostraci, Anaspida, Heterostraci). They appeared in the Middle Ordovician with two main genera of Heterostraci (*Astraspis* [FIG. 30] and *Eriptychius,* from the Harding Sandstone of Colorado) and perhaps even since the Lower Ordovician in Estonia. The jawed vertebrates or gnathostomes came to life later in the Upper Silurian, but throughout the Devonian the agnatha and true fish (belonging to the gnathostomes) coexisted.

From early to late, the successive stages of the Upper Silurian are: Caradoc, Llandovery, Wenlock, Ludlow and Downton. Of the fish, the Arthrodira would seem to have appeared in Ludlow, the Acanthodii (FIG. 90) in Wenlock. The Selachii (FIG. 89) would have been later (Middle Devonian), but the rays (*Batoidea*) have not been detected before the Lower Jurassic. The Actinopterygii (FIG. 104), that is the ray-finned fish, were thought to have appeared in the Middle Devonian but it now seems that earlier actinopterygians have been found (thanks to scales from the Gotland Ludlow level).

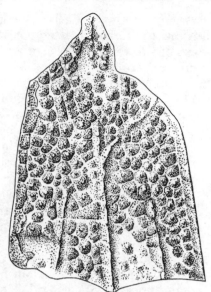

FIG. 30.—*Astraspis*: thoracic armour plate (× 3/4 app.). The first known vertebrate (from a cast).

Coelacanths appear from the beginning of the Upper Devonian in Wildungen in Germany, while the other crossopterygians—the rhipidistians (FIG. 49)—are known from the Spitzberg Lower Devonian (*Porolepis*) to the Lower Permian. The first Dipnoi also date from the Lower Devonian. In any case, no tetrapod vertebrate older than *Ichthyostega* (Greenland Upper Devonian, FIG. 50) has been discovered; tetrapod traces have also recently been observed in the Australian Upper Devonian. The stegocephalic amphibians, of which *Ichthyostega* is the first representative, persist as far as the Rhaetian (Lower Lias) stage. However, the Anura came to light at the beginning of the Triassic (*Protobatrachus*, Madagascar), whereas the much later Urodela have been found in fossil form only from the Upper Cretaceous onwards.

Since the reptiles appear in the Carboniferous, it will be useful to recall the successive stages making up the Carboniferous, from bottom to top. They are the Dinantian (= Tournaisian + Visean), Lower Westphalian or Namurian, Upper Westphalian, Stephanian. The United States Carboniferous is divided into a lower stage, the Mississippian and an upper stage, the Pennsylvanian. Reptiles appeared at the base of the Upper Carboniferous (U.S. Pennsylvanian) with various cotylosaurs (*Archerpeton, Hylonomus*). These cotylosaurs extended to the Upper Permian. The first mammalian reptiles were pelycosaurs (Upper Carboniferous—probably Nova-Scotian Westphalian—and Lower Permian in particular, but some rare pelycosaurs persisted in the Upper Permian). These mammalian reptiles were not as yet greatly differentiated. Resemblances to the mammals became more and more distinct in the course of the Triassic in the Therapsida. The Upper Triassic groups of Therapsida (Cynodonts [FIG. 84], Bauriamorphs, Tritylodonts) were the most evolved.

The first mammals (FIG. 58, 59) appear in the Lower Jurassic (Rhaetian); during the Jurassic and the Lower Cretaceous they were represented by groups with no modern equivalents; it is only at the end of the Cretaceous that the placental mammals and marsupials put in an appearance.

The other, non-mammalian inclined reptiles—the Sauropsidia—appeared, in general, later than the mammalian reptiles. The most archaic of the sauropsid groups was that of the Eosuchians, which appear to be the ancestors of the lizards. The Squamata appeared in the Triassic, but the first lacertilians, or lizards, strictly speaking, are found only from the Upper Jurassic onwards. The ophidians (snakes), in their turn, appeared in the Upper Cretaceous.

On another line of descent, the dinosaurs come to life in the middle Triassic, only to disappear in the Upper Cretaceous. The crocodilians and chelonians began in the Middle Triassic. The ichthyosaurs lasted from the Middle Triassic to the Upper Cretaceous. The plesiosauran group (Sauropterygians) has also been detected throughout the Mesozoic, from the Lower Triassic onwards. The birds, probably the most highly evolved of all sauropsids, appeared in the Upper Jurassic (Portlandian) with *Archaeopteryx* (FIG. 55).

Within the class of tertiary placental mammals we also observe the rapid disappearance of the archaic orders and the progressive appearance of the modern orders. In the Upper Cretaceous the only placentals known are insectivores such as the Mongol genera *Deltatheridium*, (FIG. 31), which is somewhat reminiscent of the shrew-mouse; *Zalambdalestes* (FIG. 32),

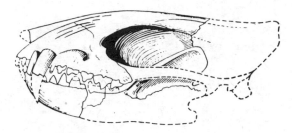

FIG. 31.—Skull of *Deltatheridium* (× 1.8). Insectivor from the Mongolian Cretaceous. (*After Simpson*)

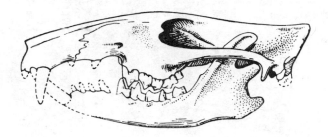

FIG. 32.—Skull of *Zalambdalestes* (× 1.4). Insectivor from the Mongolian Cretaceous. (*After Simpson*)

FIG. 33.—Procerberus (× 4), Insectivore from Montana: upper cheek teeth. (*After Sloan and Van Valen*)

placed somewhere near the hedgehogs, and *Procerberus* (FIG. 33) of Montana; and a simian *Purgatorius* (FIG. 34) from Montana. In the Palaeocene the placentals are represented by insectivores, lemurians, primitive carnivores belonging to the creodonts, Condylarthra and Amblypods.

The creodonts are carnivores whose carnassial molars are less developed than in present-day forms, or variably placed, whereas in the modern type of carnivore, still known as fissipedes, these carnassials are always the fourth upper premolar and the first lower molar. The condylarthra are defined

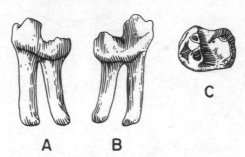

FIG. 34.—Tooth (second lower molar) of the first known primate, *Purgatorius* from the Móntana Cretaceous. (*After Van Valen*)

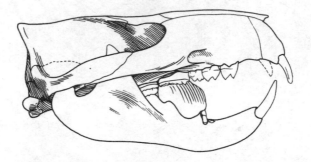

FIG. 35.—Skull of a multituberculate (*Ptilodus,* Palaeocene) (× 1.5). (*After Simpson*)

by the pulley-like articulation of two of the tarsal bones, the astragalus and the navicular bone; some have claws (*Hyopsodus,* Eocene), others have hoofs (*Phenacodus,* Palaeocene) (FIG. 36). The name Amblypoda—which does not represent a homogenous order—describes gravigrade forms with generally highly developed canines; these are subdivided into Pantodonta and Dinocerata, the latter generally having pairs of bony protuberances on the skull.

The Palaeocene deposits, characterised by a very particular fauna, with marsupials and multituberculates (FIG. 35) in addition to the placentals, are represented in Europe by only two deposits (Cernay-les-Reims and Walbeck near Halle in Germany), but by rich deposits in North America to the East of

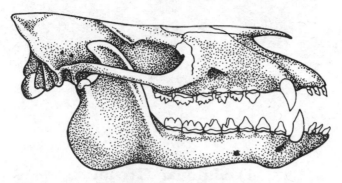

FIG. 36.—Skull of *Phenacodus* (× 1/3 app.). (*After Cope*)

the Rocky Mountains. This North American Palaeocene comprises the classical deposits of Puerco, Dragon, Torrejon,
Tiffany and Clark Fork. The European deposits correspond to
the Upper Palaeocene of the United States. In the Eocene some
of the mammals disappear (multituberculates and certain
creodonts). The marsupials persist, as do the lemurians and insectivores. But many groups appear; simians, fissipede carnivores, rodents, perissodactyls and artiodactyls,
proboscidians, edentates and cretaceans. So the Eocene looks
to us like a phase characterised by the establishment of the
principal orders of placentals although these are still
represented by forms far removed from their present
appearance. In the Oligocene the condylarths and Amblypoda
disappear and we witness the birth of a large number of
modern placental families.

   We can therefore conclude that the study of fossil
vertebrates—and of mammals in particular—proves that
various zoological groups followed one another on the surface
of the earth, generally adapting more and more strictly to
different living conditions. At the same time, many groups
failed to adapt and disappeared. The succession of fossil
vertebrates in sedimentary formations makes it necessary to
regard evolution, not as a hypothesis, but as a matter of factual
observation.

CHAPTER FIVE

Evolutionary Trends

Sometimes fossils follow one another in successively more recent geological strata, their characteristics evolving gradually and continuously. We will take as examples three particularly well-known evolutionary trends, those of the Equidae, Camelidae and Proboscidea, in each case working from the present-day representatives backward in time to the earlier predecessors. The term trend is practically synonymous with phylum. A trend should not be regarded as a linear series of successive forms but as a bushy branching of more and more recent genera.

I. The Horses

In 1839 Owen described an equid skull from the Lower Eocene (Sparnacian) found on the coast of Kent; he called this item *Hyracotherium* because he thought, wrongly, that this fossil had affinities with the hyrax. It is basically thanks to the discovery of American fossil equids that our knowledge of this family became more accurate, thanks above all to Marsh. But the earliest authors, (Cope, Matthew) regarded equid evolution as linear rather than branching.

Present-day equids are perissodactyl ungulates (with an odd

number of toes) whose body weight rests on just one toe, the third, which is median (mesaxonic). Only this single toe rests on the ground (soliped) and moreover only the tip of the toe—that is the hoof—actually touches the ground (unguligrade). This arrangement is an adaptation for running, as is the pulley arrangement of the joints of the limbs and the elongation of the various parts of the skeleton of the foot. In the pectoral arch the clavicle has disappeared and the scapula has no acromion. The ulna is fused with the radius and forms a strong olecranial apophysis. Owing to the fusion of these two bones the forearm cannot possibly rotate. The carpus is raised in relation to the ground. There are three metacarpal bones but of these, the median, or cannon-bone is much stronger than the others, which are reduced to the status of stylets. In the back leg the relatively undeveloped fibula is joined to the tibia which alone comes into contact with the twisted astragalus. The metatarsus is also represented by a third metatarsal or cannon-bone.

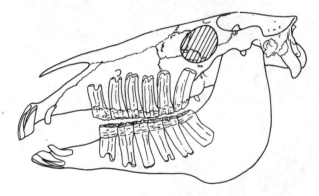

FIG. 37.—Side view of the head of living horse (molars shown with their roots).

The face of the horse (FIG. 37) is peculiarly elongated principally owing to the development of the premaxillary bone which carries the incisors; since the neck is also long, the animal is able to graze easily. The height of the face is due to the fact that the maxillaries and mandibles contain the lengthy roots of continuously growing, high-crowned (hypsodont) teeth. The dentition includes three incisors per half-jaw and six molars. The scissor-shaped incisors are high-crowned, with a small cupule of attrition, which wears away with age, so that the horse's age can be estimated by its size. Incisors and molars are separated by an interval, the bar or diastema, in which in the males only, a small, pointed canine is situated. The six molars are all the same except for the first and last, which are more triangular in shape. Of the six molars, only the first three are preceded by milk-teeth and are therefore pre-molars. All these teeth are prismatic in shape and their surface becomes worn; in old horses the tooth is ultimately worn away to the roots, which for wild horses means death. The wearing of the teeth is the result of their diet: the silica-rich grass wears away the crown of the molars; the attrition is compensated by the continuous growth of the tooth, leaving projecting crests of enamel surrounding areas of ivory and themselves surrounded by cement.

We will follow up the equid trend (FIG. 38, 39, 40, 41) proceeding from present-day forms and going back in time. This method seems more instructive, since the equids of the early Tertiary era (Eocene) were morphologically so different from present-day equids that the reader might not understand why they should be related.

The Tertiary Era comprises the following stages: Eocene, Oligocene, Miocene and Pliocene, and the Villafranchian is the lowest or earlier stage of the Quaternary. The horse which belongs to the genus *Equus* appears in the Upper Villafrachian in Europe and Asia, but perhaps a little earlier in the United States. The modern horse (*Equus caballus*) does not appear until the Recent Quaternary.

The Pliocene *Pliohippus* still has lateral digits but they are very reduced. According to the specimens, they are complete digits, with phalanges or simple bony spines alongside the cannon-bone. The dentition is very similar to that of *Equus*, but the molars are convex on the outside in this genus and straight in *Equus*.

Hipparion is a late equid (Upper Miocene and Pliocene) with three digits. Other Upper Miocene-Pliocene genera (*Neohipparion, Nannippus,* a dwarf equid) and a Quaternary genus

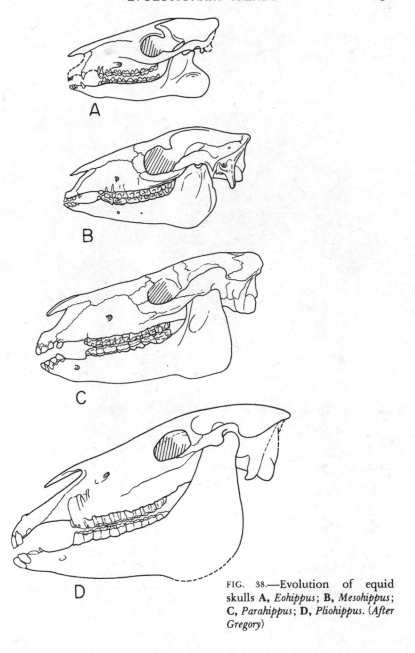

FIG. 38.—Evolution of equid skulls **A**, *Eohippus*; **B**, *Mesohippus*; **C**, *Parahippus*; **D**, *Pliohippus*. (*After Gregory*)

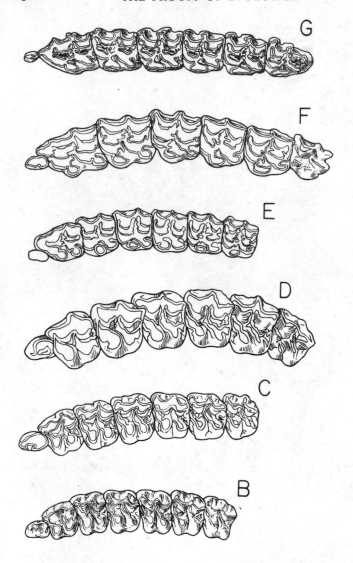

FIG. 39.—Evolution of equid
dentition A, *Eohippus*; B, *Mesohippus*; C, *Miohippus*; D, *Parahippus*;
E, *Merychippus*; F, *Pliohippus*; G,
Equus. (*After Gregory*)

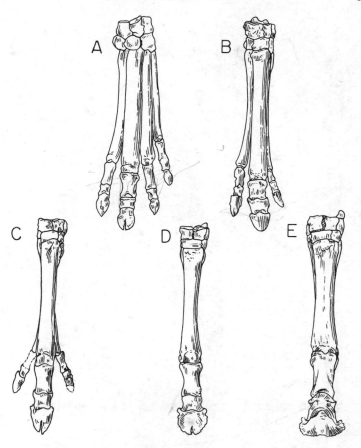

FIG. 40.—Evolution of manus of equids **A,** *Eohippus*; **B,** *Miohippus*; **C,** *Parahippus*; **D,** *Pliohippus*; **E,** *Equus.* (*After Gregory*)

(*Stylohipparion*) are placed in proximity to this fossil.

Merichippus, of the Miocene, and *Parahippus,* also of the Miocene, are equids which are close to the present-day horse and like that animal have a long muzzle, a fused ulna and radius, a fibula transformed into a long bony spine, limbs with a preponderant median digit on which the body-weight rests and high-crowned teeth (hypsodont).

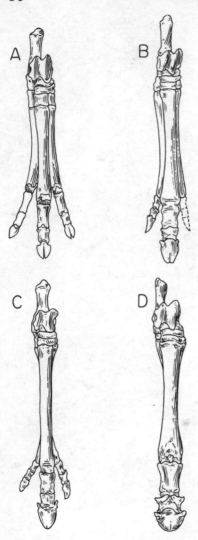

FIG. 41.—Evolution of pes of equids **A,** *Eohippus*; **B,** *Miohippus*; **C,** *Parahippus*; **D,** *Equus*. (*After Gregory*)

But the older equids do not have the hyposodont dentition. Their molars are quite low (brachiodont) and do not continue to grow. This transformation—the most important in the history of the equids—implies a change of diet: *Merychippus* and *Parahippus,* like our living horse, fed on grass, while the pre-Miocene equids ate leaves. *Mesohippus* measured only about 60 cm at the shoulder. This animal, known from some 15 excellent skeletons, dates from the Lower and Middle Oligocene. All the molars (except for the first pre-molar) have enamel crests, but of less complicated design than in more recent equids. The cusp appears for the first time in this equid. In the encephalon, which can to some extent be reconstructed thanks to endocranial casts, the cerebral hemispheres (FIG. 42B) cover the cerebellum but not the olfactory bulbs (as they do in the genus *Equus*). The front foot already has four digits, but one—the outside digit—is vestigial. The genus *Miohippus* is difficult to separate from the genus *Mesohippus* to which it is linked by transitional forms; it is distinguished by small differences in the tarsal bones. The term *Miohippus* covers the most advanced equids of the Middle Oligocene and those of the Upper Oligocene. Some leaf-eating equids such as *Archaeohippus* (Miocene), which was small, and the much bigger *Megahippus* (Pliocene) continued to exist into the Miocene and even the Pliocene epochs.

The chief Eocene equid is the celebrated *Eohippus*. This name is synonymous with *Hyracotherium*, which is the name for the same form in Europe. *Eohippus* measured 25–50 cm at the shoulder. The limbs, in which the metatarsus and metacarpus are not very long, and which have no cannon-bone, are not carried on hoofs as in the horse, but on digits under which there must have been a cushion of soft tissue. The front foot has four digits, the back three. The ulna and fibula are still quite distinct and separate from the radius and tibia respectively. The teeth, more numerous than in the living horse (44 in *Eohippus* as against 36 to 42 in the horse) have a diastema in which there is always a rather small canine. The first two, chopping premolars differ from the teeth further back, which are quite clearly low-crowned grinding teeth with six cusps.

In the encephalon, the virtually smooth hemispheres (FIG 42A) were not very substantial, but neither did the appearance of the animal resemble that of the horse in any way: *Eohippus*, with its raised hind-quarters, must have looked like a big rabbit, but one with a long, strong tail.

The other Eocene horses are anatomically very close to

Eohippus: in *Orohippus* the fourth premolar looks the same as the molars and in *Epihippus* all the premolars are comparable to molars.

The palaeontological history of the equids is always quoted as an example demonstrating evolution, but of course among the vertebrates there are other, equally indicative examples, including those of the camelids and the proboscideans.

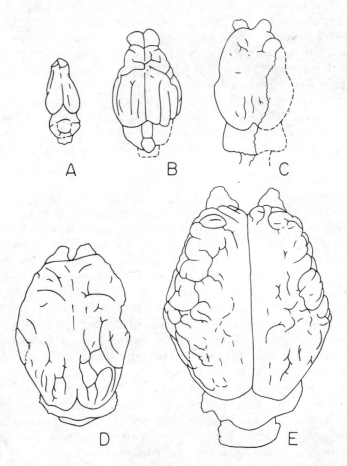

FIG. 42.—Evolution of the brain in equids **A**, *Eohippus*; **B**, *Mesohippus*; **C**, *Merychippus*; **D**, *Pliohippus*; **E**, *Equus*. (*After Ms Edinger*)

II. The Camels

The camelids are artiodactyl (even-toed) ruminants but, in contrast to the other ruminants, which are without them, they still have two upper incisors (FIG. 42); living camelids are the

FIG. 43.—Skull of camel

camels, dromedaries and llamas. These animals' lower incisors extend forward almost horizontally and meet the upper jaw, except where they lie opposite the two reduced upper incisors (in the camel the milk-teeth include three upper incisors per half-jaw). The canines are well separated from the other teeth. The quite long molars have crescent-shaped enamel crests (selenodont arrangement) but, as in horses, the teeth are hypsodont in the gazelle camels (*Stenomylinae*), a branch which has disappeared. The limbs have two digits with fused metacarpals or metatarsals (cannon-bone) and these bones diverge at the distal end; the feet do not end in hoofs but are supported on a cushion of flesh.

The fossil camelids are North American; the area of distribution of this family broke up in the Quaternary; llamas now exist only in South America, and camels in the Old World.

We shall not try at this point to trace the full history of the camelids. We shall simply list some genera which stand as landmarks in this story. The genera *Camelus* and *Llama* have been known from the Lower Quaternary (Pleistocene). *Camelops* of the North American Pleistocene is still very close to the genus *Camelus*, but this animal had a mandible with a higher horizontal branch than in the living camel. *Pliauchenia* of the North American Pliocene and *Procamelus* of the United States Upper Miocene are also genera related to *Camelus*. Like that animal, *Pliauchenia* and *Procamelus* have a long face, a gap without teeth behind the canines (diastema) and the orbit is closed by bone at the back. The limbs have a cannon-bone. But *Pliauchenia* still has three pre-molars per half-jaw and *Procamelus* four, while *Camelus* has three upper premolars and two lower premolars.

Protolabis, of the American Miocene, had relatively shorter limbs than the preceding genera; it had three upper incisors and there was no longer a cannon-bone, the metacarpals or metatarsals still being completely separated. *Protomeryx* of the Upper Oligocene and Lower Miocene in the United States has strong chopping canines, an elongated face and dental diastemas.

Poëbrotherium (North American Lower Oligocene) (FIG. 44A, B), on the other hand, is a genus whose relationship to the camelids is less obvious. It had the gait of a llama and was the size of a gazelle. Dentition was complete. The incisors were not very cutting and there was no diastema between the teeth; the orbit was still open behind. The two metacarpals (or the two metatarsals) were still separate; the muzzle was only slightly narrowed and the animal probably had hoofs.

The most important interval in the history of the camelids is between *Protomeryx* and *Poëbrotherium*. The primitive camelids must have become established in the vicinity of the genus *Protylopus* (FIG. 45) (of the Upper Eocene in the United States), which was a mammal the size of a fox with a front paw with four toes resting on the ground and two side toes, still with three phalanges, but short and non-bearing.

During the history of the camelids there has been a general increase in their size; in a side-branch, the giraffe camels, the Miocene genus *Alticamelus*, reached a height of 3.50 m. Similarly, camelid evolution is characterised by a progressive complication of the enamel coating of the molars.

III. The Elephants

The evolution of the proboscideans is equally unusually well-known, thanks specially to Osborne. Present-day

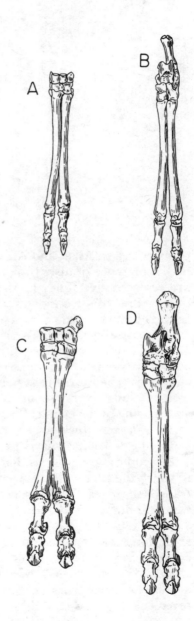

FIG. 44.—(**A, B**) *Poëbrotherium*
(United States Oligocene) and (**C,
D**) *Camelus* (**A, C**) front limb (**B,
D**) back limb. (*After Gregory*)

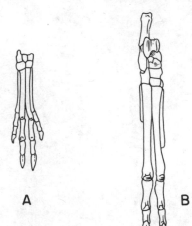

A   B   FIG. 45.—*Protylopus* (United States
Eocene) skeleton of A manus and
B pes (× 1/2 app.). (*After Scott*)

proboscideans (Asian and African elephants) are characterised
by the presence of tusks (upper incisors) and by molars which
are replaced five times in the animal's life-time. There are
never more than two molars per half-jaw at any one time. The
crown of these molars shows sub-parallel enamel ridges which
close up on themselves. The ridge has a wavy edge, enclosing
areas of dentine (ivory), with cement forming the outer edge.
This arrangement can be seen in all true living and fossil
elephants. The distinctions between these elephants (not all of
which belong to the genus *Elephas*) are based on the density
and spacing of the enamel "leaves"; For instance, in the mammoth (*Elephas primigenius*), these leaves are numerous and
serrated (FIG. 46B). So what is the origin of the elephants?

Palaeontology shows us that there were once proboscideans
in which the enamel leaves were made up of cusps arranged in
transverse ridges (the Pliocene and Pleistocene *Stegodon*) which
were still numerous (up to 13). Apart from this detail, however,
Stegodon (FIG. 46A) looked like an elephant (large size, high
skull, long upper tusks, no lower tusks, short lower jaw and
continuously growing molars). In *Stegolophodon* (from the
Upper Miocene to the Lower Quaternary), the enamel ridges
are less numerous and are made up of no more than six to
seven cusps.

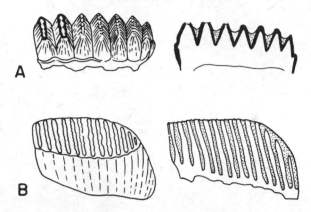

FIG. 46.—Top of molars of (A) *Stegodon*, (B) *Elephas primigenius*. (*After Boula & Piveteau*)

In the mastodons the molars have distinct cusps (as the word mastodon indicates), covered with enamel, with no cement between them. This is not the only difference between elephants and mastodons. The mastodons had shorter limbs than the elephants and longer bodies. Their skulls were low, without cavities or with poorly developed air cavities. In addition to upper tusks they often had lower tusks. But a study of fossil proboscideans has shown that the elephants followed the mastodons without interruption.

There are in fact several mastodon trends, those with a long rostrum (the longirosters) a trend comprising several phyla, and one brevirostral trend. The stegodons and stegolophodons are descended from the longirostral trend. However, certain longirosters became specialised along lines which did not produce descendants: for instance, *Rhyncotherium*, with the symphysis of the lower jaw curving downward (Upper Miocene to Pliocene), *Platybelodon* (Upper Miocene) with a shovel-shaped symphysis of the lower jaw, etc. In mastodons such as *Gomphotherium* (Upper Miocene and Pliocene)—the Sansan *Gomphotherium* or *Trilophodon angustidens* in the Gallery of Palaeontology in the Sansan Museum is a famous example—the molars have a crown in which the cusps are aligned in only a small number of ridges. *Serridentinus*, more or

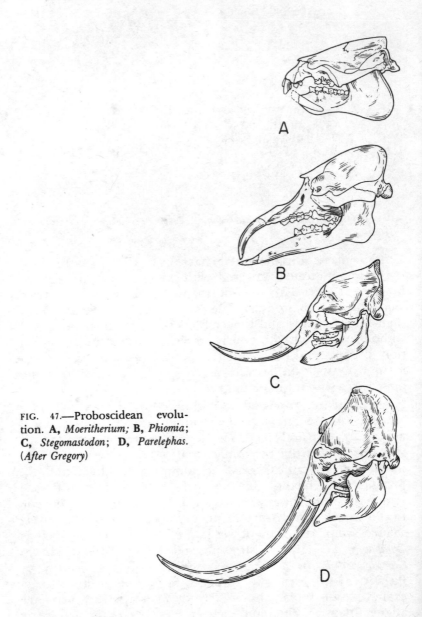

FIG. 47.—Proboscidean evolu-
tion. A, *Moeritherium;* B, *Phiomia;*
C, *Stegomastodon;* D, *Parelephas.*
(*After Gregory*)

less a contemporary of *Gomphotherium*, differs clearly from the latter, as does *Stegomastodon*, owing to the presence of small accessory cusps on the crown of the molars in addition to the main cusps.

In the history of the proboscideans, there is a long hiatus in the period between the Lower Oligocene, when the *Palaeomastodon* and *Phiomia* found at Fayum were living, and the Upper Miocene when *Gomphotherium* appeared. However, this gap in time does not go hand in hand with a morphological break, indeed the American palaeontologist Colbert regarded the genus *Gomphotherium* "as a re-edition of *Palaeomastodon* with a few improvements". *Palaeomastodon* still had small upper and lower tusks. Since the nostrils and nasal bones were placed far back on the skull, this animal probably already had a small trunk; the skull was already slightly swollen by air sinuses.

The first mastodons were rather reminiscent of another, slightly older genus from Fayum (Upper Eocene), the genus *Moeritherium* (FIG. 47A) which has only a few specialised features. In view of the rather forward position of the nostrils to the front of the snout, it is unlikely that this pig-sized animal with its massive, flat-hoofed feet, could have had a small trunk. Small upper and lower tusks were beginning to develop (one per jaw-half). The molars each had two transverse rows of two cusps.

The change in feeding patterns must have played a certain part in the evolution of the proboscideans, but only at quite a late date (Upper Pliocene), as evidenced by the wearing surfaces of the molars, on which the distinct cusps of the ridges begin to be worn on the upper face.

We could give many more examples of evolution within phyletic trends (or offshoots of such trends), but we prefer to develop the evidence by presenting examples of another kind.

CHAPTER SIX

Intermediate Forms

As we see them today, the classes of vertebrates (agnatha, fish, amphibians, reptiles, birds, mammals) appear to us to be quite distinct, but palaeontology has made it possible to discover forms which fill the gaps between most of these major groups. We will call these fossils "intermediate forms", to define organisms whose plan of organisation shows features of two groups at once, or in the case of the vertebrates examined below, of two classes. However, since we by no means know all the forms of life which have existed, we can define neither the ancestors nor the descendants of any particular fossil form with accuracy; the strict reconstruction of such a genealogical relationship is impossible, but equally, it is unimportant. The discovery of organisms which possess features peculiar to two different classes is a basic proof of evolution.

I. Origin of the Tetrapods

It was logical to seek the origin of the footed vertebrates (tetrapod vertebrates) among the fish with choanae, or internal nostrils—the Choanichthyes. What we call "choanae" are the orifices connecting the nasal fossae with the buccal cavity. Nowadays—apart from a single teleost, *Astroscopus*, which lives buried in the sand and therefore represents a very special adaptation—there are no fish with choanae; the Coelacanths do not have them and the Dipnoi have two pseudochoanae anatomically related to an external nostril. The choanichthyes therefore cover only that rhipidistian suborder of crossopterygian fish, (i.e. non-coelacanths) which lived from the Lower Devonian to the Lower Permian. These rhipidistians are now very well-known thanks to the extremely accurate description of the genus *Eusthenopteron* (Upper Devonian) by Jarvik (FIG. 49); the head of this animal (FIG. 48) has been

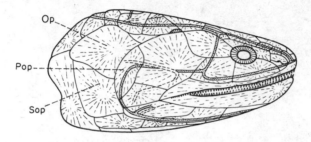

FIG. 48.—*Eusthenopteron*: Upper Devonian rhipidistian coopterygian: side view of reconstructed head (× 0.5), **Op**, opercular; **Pop**, preopercular; **Sop**, subopercular (*After Jarvik*).

studied by the method of successive polishing which has made it possible to build a very much enlarged model of the cephalic bones of this fish. The first fossil batrachians, which belong to the group of stegocephalic labyrinthodonts, have also been thoroughly studied. These forms have a highly ossified skull, are generally much bigger than living amphibians and their tooth ivory is intricately folded. All these stegocephalidae have choanae and it was logical to believe that they originated among the rhipidistians. But the hiatus between rhipidistians and stegocephalidae is considerable from the point of view of adaptation: it actually corresponds to the transition from aquatic to terrestrial life, a transformation which is probably the major stage in vertebrate evolution. Moreover the choanae probably did not always play the same role in the rhipidistians as in the tetrapods; the rhipidistians breathed through gills, the fossilised bones of the branchial skeleton have been

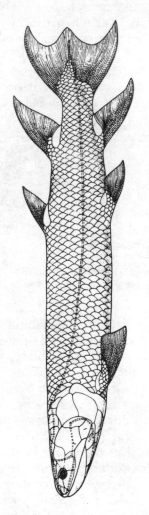

FIG. 49.—*Eusthenopteron*: reconstruction of body. (*After Jarvik*)

found—so their mouths must have been full of water, and the choanae, allowing only water to pass, must have played an essentially olfactory role, whereas the choanae of the tetrapods, which were generally gill-less, have a primarily respiratory function.

The genus *Ichthyostega*, which possesses both rhipidistian and stegocephalic features, although it was already quite distinctly a tetrapod, since it had feet, was discovered in 1931 and described for the first time in 1932 by the Swedish palaeontologist Säve Söderbergh, on the basis of fossils collected in the Old Red Sandstone of the Upper Devonian in East Greenland.

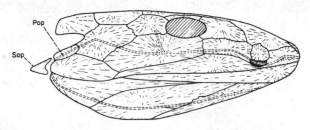

FIG. 50.—*Ichthyostega* (the first known fossil amphibian of the Upper Devonian): cheek (× 1/3 app.). (*After Jarvik*). **Pop**, preopercular; **Sop**, Subopercular.

The search for these fossils went on for about 25 years during the Danish expeditions to Greenland and after the war under the leadership of Jarvik, another Swedish palaeontologist. These expeditions succeeded in collecting more than 200 specimens.

The skull of *Ichthyostega* (FIG. 50, 51) still has a number of piscine features. While in the labyrinthodonts there are sensory grooves on the head, in the fish the corresponding feature is the sensory canals within the substance of the dermal bones. These canals prolong the lateral line system of the body along the head and contain nerve organs, the neuromasts, which are sensitive to the movement of the water. In *Ichthyostega* the bones are crossed by true sensory canals and not channelled by grooves. This feature shows that *Ichthyostega* must still have had a way of life closely linked to the aquatic environment. The cheek of *Ichthyostega* is almost identical with that of

Eusthenopteron: that is, the cheeks of these two vertebrates comprise a post-orbital, jugal, lachrymal, maxilla, quadrato-jugal and also a squamosal in which the sensory canal curves back towards the front (this canal—common to both forms—is called the jugal canal).

The acquisition of four feet was certainly connected with the disappearance of the gills; the bones which cover the gills in the fish (opercular, subopercular), no longer have a function in *Ichthyostega*; so these bones disappear (opercular) or regress, to become a scaly bone isolated in the flesh (subopercular) in *Ichthyostega*. The preopercular, a bone traversed by a sensory canal, survived in *Ichthyostega* but disappeared completely in

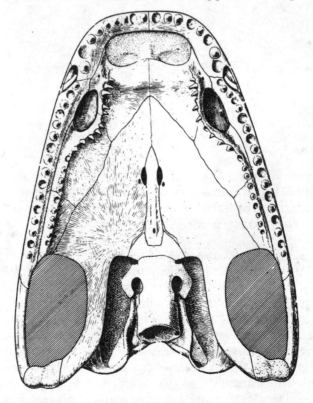

FIG. 51.—*Ichthyostega*; ventral view of skull (× 1/2 app.). (*After Jarvik*)

the other labyrinthodonts. The external nostril occupies a special position along the upper edge of the mouth between premaxilla and maxilla. This is a specialised feature which shows that *Ichthyostega* is not a strictly intermediate organism between rhipidistians and labyrinthodonts; the palaeontologists have in fact noted that the characteristics of organisms did not often evolve at the same rate (mosaic evolution). The roof of the skull in *Ichthyostega* is specially characterised, by comparison with that of *Eusthenopteron*, by the recession of the pineal orifice; this is a labyrinthodont skull roof, but the interpretation of the bones is disputed. The median bone of the palate (FIG. 51), the parasphenoid, is short as it is in *Eusthenopteron* and, as also in the fish, the palate bones are barely separated from the parasphenoid (epipterygoid, entopterygoid, dermopalatines, vomers).

In the lower jaw (FIG. 50) the external surface bones (dentary and four infradentary bones), of the internal (prearticular) and of the upper surface (three coronoids) exist in both *Ichthyostega* and *Eusthenopteron*. The brain pan of *Ichthyostega* was divided

A   B

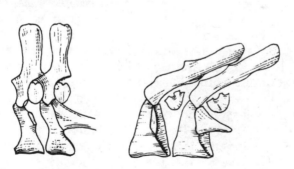

FIG. 52.—Structure of vertebrae: **A**, *Ichthyostega*; **B**, *Eusthenopteron*. (*After Jarvik*)

into two parts, one anterior, the other posterior, articulated one above the other as in *Eusthenopteron*, but in contrast to that rhipidistian, *Ichthyostega* already has an occipital condyle—in fact a double one where the head joins the spinal column.

The spinal columns (FIG. 52) of *Ichthyostega* and *Eusthenopteron* have the same structure: under a well-developed neural arch there is an anterior vertebral element, the intercentrum, followed posteriorly by a more reduced element, the pleurocentrum, indented by notches in which the dorsal and ventral roots of the spinal nerve must have lain (an arrangement known as rachitoma).

The unpaired fins of *Ichthyostega* have not yet completely disappeared and this animal still has a continuous caudalo-dorsal unpaired fin. The presence of this fin confirms that *Ichthyostega*'s way of life was still largely aquatic. Other, more advanced labyrinthodonts than *Ichthyostega* may have fins, but *Ichthyostega*'s caudalo-dorsal fin is peculiar, because it has a structure comparable to that of a rhipidistian unpaired fin, with endo-skeletal rays and dermal rays inserted between them and projecting beyond them on the outside. The simultaneous presence of a fin and feet in *Ichthyostega* demonstrates the intermediate character of this labyrinthodont, which still has fins, though in regression, but whose feet are already powerful.

The problem of the origin of the limbs of tetrapod vertebrates has been the subject of much debate and has recently been resolved thanks to an accurate description of the internal skeleton of the pectoral fin of *Eusthenopteron*. This skeleton (FIG. 53A) comprises a humerus, a radius and an ulna; a digit I and an ulnar are attached to the ulna, the ulnar itself having four digits. This internal skeleton represents a true miniature arm, elements of which are found in the labyrinthodonts. Unfortunately in *Ichthyostega* the osteology of the front limb is not thoroughly known and the "arm" of *Eusthenopteron* has to be compared with the back limb of *Ichthyostega* (FIG. 53B). In this the femur is the posterior equivalent to the humerus, the tibia corresponding to the radius, the fibula to the ulna, but there are seven digits represented by a series of bones. In *Eusthenopteron* the internal skeleton of the pectoral fin also comprises seven distal but undivided elongations. The transformation of the internal skeleton of the pectoral fin of *Eusthenopteron* into a tetrapod limb implies the division of these elongations and the formation of digits. Note also that the humerus of *Ichthyostega* already has an olecranial apophysis ("funny-bone").

So we can see that *Ichthyostega* has features of both

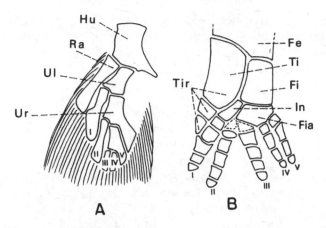

FIG. 53.—Comparison of the back limb of **B** *Ichthyostega* and the internal skeleton **A** *Eusthenopteron* of the pectoral fin of **Ul**, ulna; **Ur**, ulnare; **Fe**, femur; **Hu**, humerus; **In**, intermedium, **Fi**, fibula; **Fia**, Fibulare; **Ra**, radius; **Tir**, tibial ray; **Ti**, tibia; I, II, III, IV, V, digits 1–5

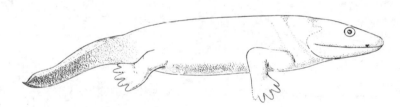

FIG. 54.—*Ichthyostega:* reconstruction (× 1/10 app.). (*After Jarvik*)

rhipidistians and labyrinthodonts and that thanks to this fossil we can understand how the vertebrates were able to desert their aquatic environment and gradually adapt to a terrestrial one (FIG. 54).

The conquest of the land does not mean that a primitive fish "chose" to go exploring on land, where he could only move in awkward hops and that the acquisition of tetrapod limbs was the result of a modification of behaviour as M. J. Monod claims. Jarvik has in fact shown that the limb of *Eusthenopteron* (internal skeleton of the pectoral) existed *before* it left the water, and was pre-adapted to territorial conquest.

Ichthyostega represents a link in the evolutionary chain between fish and tetrapods; however, it is certain that other attempts to leave the water took place, about which we know very little as yet.

II. "Archaeopteryx"

The most famous genus of intermediate vertebrates between two classes is still *Archaeopteryx*; this is the example almost always quoted in the elementary treatises because historically this already old discovery is very important. It proved beyond any argument that there was an animal—*Archaeopteryx*— which had both reptilian and bird features. Even the circumstances of the discovery were perhaps not unconnected with the fame of this fossil.

In 1861, in the Upper Jurassic lithographic stone of Bavaria (Solenhofen Portlandian, to be more precise: the Langenaltheimer Haardt area), Dr. Häberlein found a fossil *Archaeopteryx*. This fossil (with some more of the same provenance) was sold for £700 to the British Museum, the payment providing a dowry for Dr. Häberlein's daughter. A second specimen was discovered near Eichstedt in 1877 and the Humboldt University Museum in Berlin was able to buy it for 20,000 marks owing to the generosity of a rich patron, Siemens. These two classic specimens in the museums in London and Berlin certainly belong to the same genus and the same species (*Archaeopteryx lithographica*). A third *Archaeopteryx* was found in 1956 in a quarry in Langenaltheimer Haardt (250 m. from the place where the London specimen had been found and at a level 6–8 m higher); this specimen, which was less well-preserved than the first two, was described by F. Heller in 1958 and is at Erlangen University. A fourth, very fragmentary specimen comprising only the imprints of the limbs, girdle and a few feathers was found in 1970 in the Haarlem museum collections by the American palaeontologist Ostrom. A fifth *Archaeopteryx*, smaller than the previous specimens, has been extracted from the Bavarian deposit (Mayr 1973). So we now have five specimens of *Archaeopteryx*.

In the Kimmeridgian of Lerida (near Barcelona) the feathers

of isolated birds have often been described; in themselves, these seem of dubious value.

In any case, the hiatus between reptiles and birds is much less wide than the one which separates the crossopterygians from the amphibians and in this sense *Archaeopteryx* seems to be a less conclusive example than *Ichthyostega*. Flight is not in fact the exclusive prerogative of birds; there have been flying reptiles (pterosaurs) and nowadays birds appear to be more of a special branch of the sauropsid reptiles (reptiles with a straight fourth branchial arch, in contrast to mammals, for instance).

Archaeopteryx (FIG. 55) is closer to the reptiles than to the birds:

1. The bones are not pneumatic. In the bird, the bone is very thin and perforated by openings carrying the air from

FIG. 55.—Skeleton of *Archaeopteryx*: reconstruction. Black areas are those which differ most from the skeleton of a living bird. (× 0.14). (*After Colbert*)

the lungs into the air vacuities within the bone. *Archaeopteryx's* bones are actually quite thin but perforations have never been observed. The Archaeopteryx bone is not truly pneumatic.

2. The mouth possesses well-developed teeth.

3. The axial skeleton shows amphicoelous (hollow-ended) vertebrae without the saddle articulation of living birds. The sacrum comprises six vertebrae (there are 11–23 sacral vertebrae in birds). This axial skeleton ends in a long tail with well-separated vertebrae, which is not found in birds, where the tail is represented by a single bone in the shape of a plough-share, the pygostyle.

4. The ribs were slender, not articulated to the sternum, and lacked uncinated processes (antero-posterior processes attached to the ribs and reinforcing the thoracic cage; these hooked processes exist only in birds). The sternum lacks completely the features of a breast-bone.

5. Ventral ribs (*gastralis*) existed in the ventral section of the trunk and their presence is incompatible with flight. They therefore do not occur in birds.

6. In the limbs, the metacarpals are generally free, whereas in birds these bones are joined to each other and to the carpals. The fingers end in claws; this reptilian feature (the presence of some claws) is in fact found in some birds such as the hoatzin and the rail. In the leg, the fibula is not reduced in relation to the tibia (in contrast to the avian arrangement). The metatarsals are independent (at least to a certain extent, and as in the reptiles). However, there seem to be differences in this respect according to the specimens: for instance, although the metatarsals are separated in the London and Berlin specimens they seem to be fused proximally in the Erlangen specimen. In living birds, on the other hand, there is a tarsometatarsal joined to a single tibio-tarsal.

However, *Archaeopteryx* also possesses undeniable avian features: first of all the arms had feathers (remiges, or wing-quills) as did the tail (rectrices, or tail-quills). These feathers have the same structure as those of living birds, with a rachis, or spine bearing barbs, tipped in their turn by barbules.

Some of the osteological features are also avian. For instance, the fusion of the two clavicles in a single wish-bone as in birds, and the presence of a pubis elongated towards the back.

Archaeopteryx must still have flown very badly, with its unkeeled sternum, rigid neck and weak rib-cage without hooked processes, but with, on the other hand, ventral ribs preventing the strong musculature needed for flight. Since the wing surface was considerable (long, feathered tail), the animal must also have found it difficult to manoeuvre. These conditions are confirmed by a study of the natural brain cast discovered by de Beer on the London specimen; on this cast the optic lobes and cerebellum are less well-developed than their corresponding imprints in living birds (the brain cast of birds corresponds accurately to the structure of their brain). So the cerebral structure of *Archaeopteryx* was also distinctly reptilian.

III. The Double Articulation of the Lower Jaw

It was long assumed that the transformation of reptiles into mammals occurred very abruptly. It seemed, in fact, that the reptiles, with a lower jaw making a joint with a bone of branchial origin, the quadrate, were quite different from mammals, in which the articulation of the lower jaw takes place between two morphologically more external bones, the dentary, on the lateral surface of the lower jaw and the squamosal, a cranial bone. Since the end of the war it has been shown that there were many vertebrates which had both the quadrate articular joint of the reptiles and the squamoso-dentary mammalian joint. Are these vertebrates, some of which are often called *Eotheria*, mammals or reptiles? As we have already seen, the transformation of the therapsid reptiles into mammals is extremely gradual and the attribution of the intermediate form to one class or the other is completely subjective. The study of these evolved mammal-like reptiles is one of the great achievements—and a very recent one—of modern palaeontology.

We shall arbitrarily define mammals as being characterised

by the presence of squamoso-dentary joints, on the understanding that mammals may also possess in addition to this a quadrate-articular joint and that the distinction between mammalian reptiles and mammals is artificial.

The double articulation of the lower jaw has been described: 1. In a Middle Triassic therapsid of the cynodont order, *Probainognathus*, where it is only in the process of becoming differentiated; 2. in a mammalian reptile of the South African Stormberg Level (equivalent to the European Upper Triassic and Rhaetic), in which the joint is double but very specialised (*Diarthrognathus*); 3. in a Rhaetic (Lower Lias) mammal from Wales (*Morganucodon*) and from the Chinese Upper Triassic; 4. in a mammal from the redbeds (Rhaetian) of Basutoland (Lesotho), *Erythrotherium*; and 5. in a pantotherian mammal of the Welsh Rhaetic, *Kuehneotherium*. We shall study these genera one by one.

1. *Probainognathus* comes from the Middle Triassic of northern Argentina (deposit of the Rio Chañares in Rioja Province). This genus, discovered by the American palaeontologist

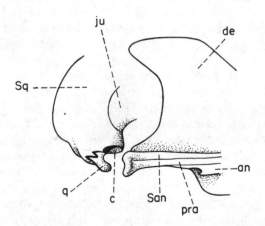

FIG. 56.—A mammalian reptile with the beginnings of squamoso-dentary articulation, Probainognathus (× 1.7 app.). (*After Romer*); **an**, angular; **c**, cavity where squamosal articulates with quadrate; **de**, dentary; **ju**, jugal; **pra**, prearticular; **q**, quadrate; **San**, surangular: **Sq**, squamosal

Romer, belongs to the family of the Chiniquodontidae, an advanced group of the cynodont order. Cynodonts are mammalian reptiles with a secondary palate separating the nasal fossae from the mouth and with highly advanced dentition. In the Chiniquodontidae the secondary palate is particularly extended towards the back. In *Probainognathus* (FIG. 56) the quadrate is a small bony element situated rather loosely in a double indentation of the squamosal. The reduced articular formed the posterior portion of a fixed lamina on the medial face of the dentary. This lamina comprised a further three bones (angular, surangular and prearticular). In the other chiniquodonts the dentary did not reach the squamosal, but as the quadrate joint was weak it is probable that dentary and squamosal were already playing a part in the articulation of the lower jaw by means of connecting ligaments.

But in *Probainognathus* there are traces of the true mammalian articulation: on the postero-inferior surface of the squamosal there is a very well-defined cavity in which the posterior end of the dentary must have been situated. This is the initial stage of the formation of mammalian articulation. Thanks to Professors Romer and Crompton I had the opportunity of seeing *Probainognathus* at Harvard and I would like to thank them here for their kindness. There is no doubt about the existence of the squamosal cavity described by Romer. One might also think of it as an insertion site for an articular ligament, but I agree with Romer that it is more likely to have been used for the insertion of the dentary, its outline is so clear and well-defined. Romer comments that in these circumstances *Probainognathus* must be regarded as a mammal, if mammals are defined by the presence of squamoso-dentary articulation, whereas the three other known genera of chiniquodonts are reptiles according to the classical lower jaw criterion. This would bring the reptile–mammal boundary into one family, the Chiniquodontidea.

As we can see, the criterion of the lower jaw joint becomes absurd at this point: *Probainognathus* is in fact a chiniquodontid in every feature and although the mammals may have originated with this genus, still it is undoubtedly a cynodont. In these circumstances it is obviously no longer possible to define mammals by the single feature of the squamoso-dentary joint of the lower jaw, all mammals do possess this joint, but they also have a peculiar dentition with cusped postcanines and two sets of teeth (milk and permanent) and the volume of the cavity within the cranium is large.

The example of *Probainognathus* and the Chiniquodontidae shows us that the mammalian lower jaw joint was acquired gradually. As the quadrate-articular joint weakened a compensatory mechanism had to come into operation to enable the lower jaw to continue to play its part, hence the appearance of the squamoso-dentary joint. Several stages marking this transformation have been observed. For instance, in the cynodont *Thrinaxodon* of South Africa a knob can be seen on the ventral edge of the squamosal in the articular area. This knob, quite close to the postero-dorsal edge of the surangular, must have been in contact with that bone or joined to it by ligaments.

2. *Diarthrognathus* is a fossil which was described in 1929 by Broom (the author's Ictidosaurian B), but which has only recently been fully understood thanks to the descriptions by

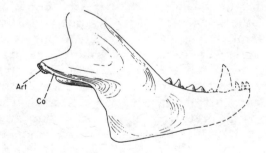

FIG. 57.—A vertebrate with double articulation of the lower jaw: *Diarthrognathus* (× 1.25). (*After Crompton*): **Art,** articular; **Co,** condyle.

Crompton (1958, 1963). Broom had already noted that the cranium of this genus was highly evolved, observing in particular that "the dentary could easily form a new joint with the squamosal which it must almost already have touched".

Crompton showed that this fossil (FIG. 57) did have a double-jointed lower jaw:

(a) The posterior wall of the dentary should normally be in contact with the squamosal, although the dentary did not yet have an articular condyle. However, a thick fold of the external face of the dentary presents a pock-marked surface, the trace of a covering of cartilage which proves that there was a true joint with cartilage between the squamosal and dentary rather than a simple contact.

(b) Reptilian articulation was of a special type with a concave articular surface of the quadrate in contrast to the rule (and correspondingly that of the articular was convex). But this interpretation has been disputed by Kermack, who thinks that what Crompton regards as the articular is really a quadrate.

Whatever interpretation is given to the bones to the back of the lower jaw, all authors agree that a reptilian joint is present. Should one therefore regard *Diarthrognathus* as a mammal or as an advanced reptile related to the bauriamorphs (mammalian reptiles with non-specialised teeth, a secondary palate and no post-orbital bar)? The same type of problem arises with *Diarthrognathus* as with *Probainognathus*.

3. *Morganucodon* (still called *Eozostrodon*, the name which actually has priority and is regarded as the correct one) has always been considered to be undeniably a mammal. In 1939 Kühne defined the genus *Eozostrodon* on the basis of two Rhaetic molars from Somerset. In 1949 Kühne discovered a molar from a Welsh quarry to which he gave the name *Morganucodon* (the material was not sufficient to confirm that it was identical with Parrington's genus). This tooth was found in the Rhaetic limestone fissure filling in carboniferous rocks. In 1951 Kühne excavated the back of a lower jaw-bone from the same quarry. Then, in 1955, Kermack and Mussett extracted the remains of several thousand individuals from the Pant quarry, also in Wales and also containing Rhaetic limestone. Other remains of *Morganucodon* were found in the Yunnan in

1948 by Oehler and briefly described by Rigney in 1963. The deposit, which also provided an advanced mammalian reptile, genus *Bienotherium*, is of the Upper Triassic. The British species has been called *Morganucodon watsoni*; the Chinese one *Morganucodon oehleri*.

The dentary condyle is visible in *Morganucodon watsoni*, which is therefore a mammal. The dentary has a high coronoid process (FIG. 58). On the inner face of the jaw and towards the

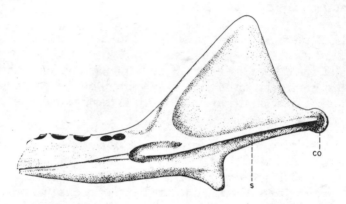

FIG. 58.—A mammal which still has the quadrate-articular jaw joint, *Morganucodon* (× 0.8). (*After Kühne*): s, *sulcus cartilaginis meckeli*; co, condyle.

back there is a depression. A similar depression has been found in the tritylodont mammalian reptile *Oligokyphus*. In *Oligokyphus*, a Rhaetic genus from Wales like *Morganucodon*, this depression, called the *sulcus cartilaginis meckeli*, was the site of the very reduced bones of the back of the jaw, in particular the angular and the articular, and the jaw-joint was reptilian. Kermack and Musset therefore very logically conclude from the presence of the *sulcus cartilaginis meckeli* in *Morganucodon watsoni* that this species must, in addition to the mammalian jaw articulation, have possessed a reptilian articulation of the lower jaw. These authors suggested that the mammals with this double joint which retained the reptilian articulation should be classed as *Eotheria* (a new group). In reality it seems that the mammalian articulation must have appeared in various phyla and the *Eotheria* class does not appear to be valid in the light of recent discoveries. In any case the expectations of Kermack and Musset were verified in *Morganucodon oehleri*. The reptilian jaw articulation, according to Rigney, is actually present in *Morganucodon oehleri*, which differs from *Morganucodon watsoni* in having larger postcanines and a different dental formula.

The lower jaw of the genus *Docodon* from the Morrisson formation (Upper Jurassic, Wyoming) has molars which differ from those of *Morganucodon*, but the lower jaw also has a large *sulcus cartilaginis meckeli*. It is therefore probable that this genus also had both types of joint.

4. *Erythrotherium* (FIG. 59) has been described only on the basis of an isolated lower jaw, by Crompton in 1964 (but a skull has also been excavated which has not yet been studied). As in *Morganucodon* and *Docodon*, in addition to the articular condyle

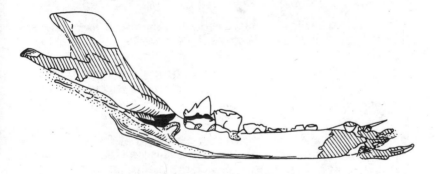

FIG. 59.—A Rhaetic mammal from Basutoland which probably had a jaw with double articulation: *Erythrotherium* (× 4). (*After Crompton*).

of the dentary, there is a groove on the median face of the jaw in which bony splinters can be seen which correspond to the bones of the reptilian jaw joint. (However, it is not apparent that the reptilian joint was truly functional in this genus.) Unfortunately, the systematic affinities of *Ertythrotherium* are not clear.

The Orange State Jurassic genus *Tritylodontoideus* also had both types of joint, according to Fourie. But the bones themselves in this fossil have not been preserved and although the interpretation is plausible it seems less certain than in the previous cases.

5. All the forms briefly described above were discovered recently and were difficult to place in the classically known secondary orders of mammals. The new genus *Kuehneotherium* found by Kermack and Musset in the Welsh Rhaetic, on the other hand, is a pantothere, according to the authors. In this order the crown of the molars generally possesses three cusps arranged in a triangle, but in certain molars a fourth cusp joins the first three: this is the talonid. We know *Kuehneotherium*

FIG. 60.—A pantotherian mammal from the Welsh Rhaetic; lower jaw with double articulation: *Kuhneotherium* (× 5). (*After Kermack*)

through only one jaw-bone with a coronoid process (FIG. 60), but without the postero-inferior angular process found in *Morganucodon* and *Docodon*. *Kuehneotherium* also had a *sulcus cartilaginis meckeli* and therefore probably had at least a vestigial lower jaw articulation.

All these are recent observations showing that, far from being incompatible, the two jaw articulations, mammalian and reptilian, were able to survive together in quite a number of archaic mammals belonging to various trends. Both in this and in other regards, intermediate forms between mammalian reptiles and mammals do exist.

CHAPTER SEVEN

Human Palaeontology and Evolution

It has only recently been accepted that fossil men actually existed who differed from living man (*Homo sapiens*) and preceded him. In Cuvier's view both man and monkeys appeared after the last revolution of the globe and in these circumstances fossil primates could not have differed from living forms. This was, in fact, a rather curious claim, since Cuvier already knew one fossil lemur, *Adapis*, from the Paris Basin Eocene, but he regarded *Adapis* as a "pachyderm" rather than a lemur.

Gradually, 19th century discoveries undermined Cuvier's claims. First of all, in 1834, a fossil monkey, *Pliopithecus*, was found by Edouard Lartet in the Miocene of the Aquitaine Basin (Sansan). Then fossil human beings were discovered, beginning with the skull of Neanderthal Man (1856) and its visibly archaic features, followed by the La Naulette mandible (1965). The outstanding feature of La Naulette was the absence of chin, which showed that it belonged to a human branch differing from *Homo sapiens*. Finally, in 1891, the first remains of *Pithecanthropus* were dug up in Java by a Dutch army doctor, Eugene Dubois. He was convinced that man, lacking a covering of hair, could only have appeared in tropical countries, and had asked for an appointment in Indonesia to enable him to carry out research on fossil men. Dubois called the human fossils of Java which he discovered *Pithecanthropus*, a name which Haeckel had originally given to a hypothetical intermediate form, between the higher apes and man.

As we know, Darwin's famous statement that "man is descended from the monkey" gave rise to furious controversy. But the great anthropoid apes (gorilla, chimpanzee, orangutan, gibbon) are quite distinct from man in a number of features, such as the appearance of the teeth, the anatomy of the foot, the relative proportions of the length of limbs (the apes have long arms and short legs, the converse of the human adaptation). It now appears that man could not have descended from the great anthropoid apes. The human strain must have formed a separate branch a very long time ago. The animal origins of man do not seem to be in doubt, however. And it is undoubtedly to Darwin that we owe this revelation. But human features must have appeared far sooner than was believed—even as early as the Tertiary era.

It is true that we have no evidence of a Tertiary man, but a large Tertiary primate, *Oreopithecus* (FIG. 61) is much closer to man than the living anthropoids. *Oreopithecus* comes from the Pontian lignite of Tuscany (Upper Miocene). Fragments of this animal's skeleton were studied by Gervais in 1870 and recently the Swiss palaeontologist Hürzeler has resumed study of *Oreopithecus* fossils in the museums and succeeded in putting together a complete skeleton of the animal. This *Oreopithecus* (FIG. 62), despite its great age (some fifteen million years), had a humanoid set of teeth with small canines, vertical incisors and no gap (diastema) between incisors and canines. The face was short, with no muzzle. The pelvis, as in man, was not very high (whereas the pelvis of the big apes is shaped like an elongated lamina) and its form is one generally associated with bipeds. But *Oreopithecus'* arms were proportionally very long and it must have been able to move by swinging from the branches (brachiation). Because of this feature, in particular, it is improbable that *Oreopithecus* could belong to the same line as man. It probably represents the vestiges of a small branch parallel to the human branch itself. Nevertheless its existence

But a large Tertiary Primate, Oreopithecus is much closer to Man than the living anthropoids.

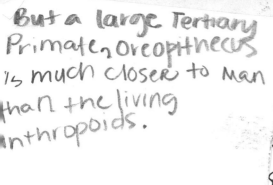

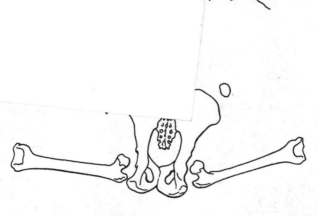

FIG. 61.—Pelvis of (*above*) Oreopithecus and (*below*) Chimpanzee. The pelvis of *Oreopithecus*, much wider than that of the Chimpanzee, indicates that *Oreopithecus* was already bipedal. (*After Piveteau*)

demonstrates the great palaeontological age of the various features of living man. In fact, in the Baringo Deposit (Kenya) Bishop has also just discovered a humaroid molar crown ten million years old.

The experts do not agree even on a definition of man. Such a definition is dependent on criteria which are partially subjective. Nevertheless, all the authors agree in placing *Australopithecus*, *Pithecanthropus* and Neanderthal man in the human line of descent or close to it. These human or humanoid types do represent a continuous series and human palaeontology therefore supplies us with one of the most remarkable proofs of evolution. These results have only been obtained recently: *Australopithecus* was discovered in 1925, Pekin man (*Sinanthropus*) between 1927 and 1937. This is

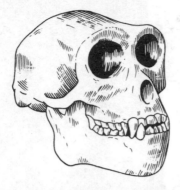

FIG. 62.—Skull of *Oreopithecus*.
(*After Hürzelen*)

probably one of the reasons why these new data of human palaeontology are rarely quoted as proofs of evolution. *Australopithecus* (FIG. 63) has been found in South Africa and in

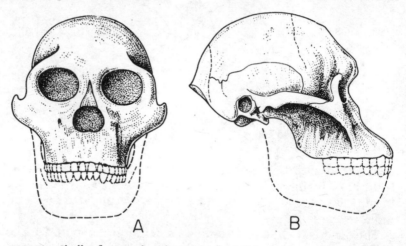

A   B

FIG. 63.—Skull of Australopithecus (*Australopithecus sensu stricto*). **A**, front view; **B**, side view. (*After Broom and Robinson*)

East Africa (Tanzania and Ethiopia). These creatures still had a number of simian features: the brain-case capacity was small, between 400 and 600 cm³. The face was prognathous with the characteristic appearance of a snout. The skull was low, the brow receding. The eye ridge was heavy. All these simian characteristics are, however, less notable than in the apes. But the australopithecines are human in other respects:

(1) The occipital opening of the skull was on the horizontal plane, a feature related to the upright posture.

(2) As in man, the canines did not protrude beyond the level of the other teeth, the incisors were vertical, not procumbent.

(3) The pelvis was shaped like a wide plate as in man, not the protracted leaf-shape seen in the apes. The shape of this pelvis (FIG. 66) shows that the australopithecines must have been used to standing on their back legs. This argument corroborates the first, confirming that the posture of the australopithecines was upright.

Nevertheless, the dental arcade (FIG. 68) was in the shape of a long U and the molars were very powerful. These two features are not, of course, found in man.

In all the australopithecines we find two basic forms. There is a slender form (FIG. 63) with a moderately developed supra-orbital (eyebrow) ridge and without a sagittal crest. This is *Hustralopithecus* in the strict sense. And there is also "brute" form with a heavy supra-orbital ridge and a sagittal crest, known as *Paranthropus* (FIG. 64). The *Paranthropus* type includes,

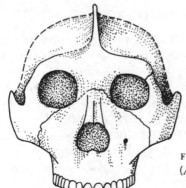

FIG. 64.—Skull of *Paranthropus*. (*After Broom and Robinson*)

in addition to the South African Paranthropus, *Zinjanthropus* (FIG. 65) from Tanzania and some lower jaw-bones from the Omo basin (Ethiopia) described under the name of

Paraustralopithecus (FIG. 70, Arambourg and Coppens). *Paranthropus* is undoubtedly very old. A temporal was recently discovered in the Baringo deposit and is estimated to be four million years old. The oldest jaw-bone of *Paraustralopithecus* has been put at 2½ million years old. *Zinjanthropus* from Tanzania, on the other hand, probably lived 1,700,000 years ago. The most recent *Paranthropus* is probably only a million years old (Baringo deposit).

Moreover, *Australopithecus* was already a tool-user with a primitive stone industry. He also used bone for tool-making. However, we do not know if *Paranthropus* also practised these industries.

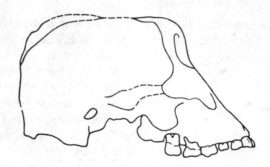

FIG. 65.—Skull of *Zinjanthropus*. (*After Le Gros Clark*)

The most ancient *Pithecanthropus* dates from some 700,000 years ago, (Although the estimates made on this subject are debatable, the order of magnitude is probably fairly accurate.) The *Pithecanthropus* group includes Java man, *Sinanthropus* from China (the ones from Pekin and the one from Shensi), *Atlanthropus* from Ternifine near Oran, and the "men" of Rabat and Casablanca. Other forms such as the South African *Telanthropus*, certain men from Olduvai (Tanzania) and *Chadanthropus* were probably ancient types of *Pithecanthropus* or forms slightly more archaic than *Pithecanthropus*.

It would have been convenient to group these human types which are to some extent intermediate between *Australopithecus* and *Pithecanthropus* under the name of *Homo habilis*: but the fossils designated *Homo habilis* are not at all homogeneous. It would not therefore be possible to call "*Homo habilis*" a specific stage. It is true that this is a group of forms in human evolution which passed beyond the stage of *Australopithecus* but had not yet attained that of *Pithecanthropus*.

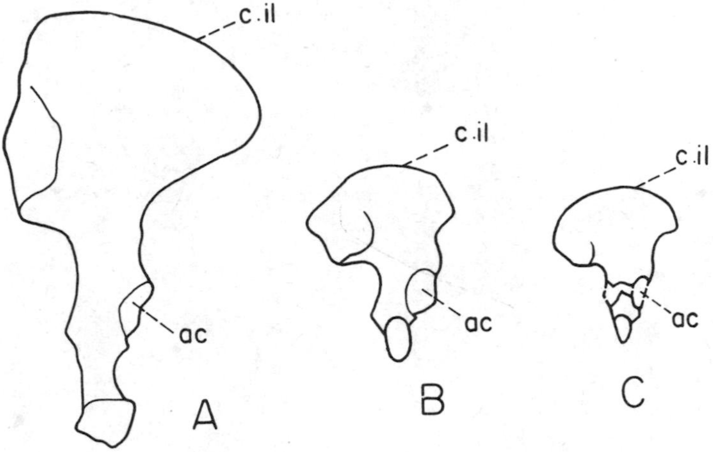

FIG. 66.—Comparison of the pelvis of (**A**) Chimpanzee, (**B**) living man and (**C**) an Australopithecine; **ac**, acetabulum receiving the head of the femur; **c, il**, iliac crest. (*After Le Gros Clark*)

In *Pithecanthropus* (FIG. 67) the capacity of the brain-case was about 1,000 cm³. The skull was flat, the brow receding. The supra-orbital ridge was massive and there was great post-orbital constriction. The cranial wall was thick, the nasal bones were large and flat, while the jaw-bone, which was parabolic but not truncated towards the front, was sturdy. In the dentition, the canines did not protrude beyond the other teeth. Pithecanthropus differed from living man above all in his more powerful jaw and less capacious brain case.

Finally, Neanderthal man represents a much more recent stage in human evolution than pithecanthropus. He appeared during the last glaciation, known as the Würm glaciation (probably about 70,000 years ago). The man found at La Chapelle-aux-Saints (Corrèze) (FIG. 69) has been particularly well-described by Boule. Only 1.55 meters tall, his head was capacious with a very high cranial capacity (1,625 cm³), larger

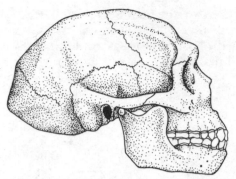

FIG. 67.—Reconstruction of skull of Sinanthropus. (*After Weinart*)

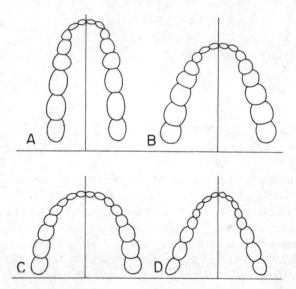

FIG. 68.—Various forms of dental arcade in the Hominids: **A,** squared parabolic (Australopithecine); **B,** parabolic (Pithecanthropian); **C,** squared parabolic (Neanderthalian); **D,** parabolic (*Homo sapiens*). (*After Mme Genet Varcin*)

than that of *Homo sapiens*. The large volume of the brain case was due to its elongated shape at the back. The brow receded, the face was more prognathous than in living man. The mandibular arcade was parabolic and truncated towards the front,

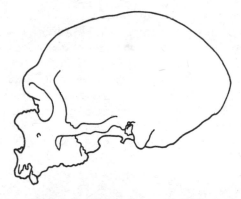

FIG. 69.—Side view of the skull of Chapelle-aux-Saints man. (*After Boule*)

but short. The thigh bones were markedly curved and the foot must still have been prehensile. Nevertheless, some neanderthaloids, for instance the one from Israel, have less archaic features than most of the men of this group. Of course there are also archaic hominids such as Rhodesian man and Solo man which are neither *Homo sapiens* nor neanderthaloids.

All these human forms succeed one another so perfectly that

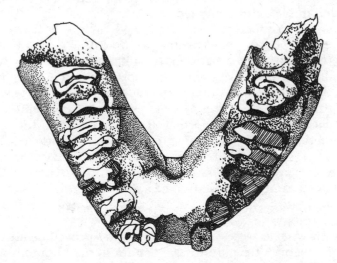

FIG. 70.—Lower jaw of *Paraustralopithecus* seen from above. (*Unpublished drawing kindly contributed by Yves Coppens*)

writers on this subject cannot agree on the nature of the predecessors of the human strain. If we adhere to a purely psychological criterion—tool-making—then australopithecines are men. This extreme position, according to which *Australopithecus* in the strict sense would be attached to the genus *Homo* and belong to the species *Homo transvalensis*, has not been generally accepted. On the contrary, most authors do class *Pithecanthropus* as a man, *Homo erectus*. This difficulty of classification is simply the result of the continuity of succession of human fossil forms.

Moreover, it is clear that these stages in human evolution—*Australopithecus, Pithecanthropus*, Neanderthal man—do not comprise a single trend. They are more like a family tree, some of whose branches advance towards the three main structural stages. But there is a difficulty: anatomically speaking—apart, of course, from the quite fundamental development of the brain itself—*Homo sapiens* does not seem to have evolved a great deal. For instance, his dentition is very simple and primitive. It is difficult to understand how forms which are morphologically very specialised could give rise to living man who, in various respects, seems anatomically simpler and less differentiated.

Human evolution can be explained on the basis of two different hypotheses: according to Madame Genet-Varcin, man represents the very ancient culmination of a phylogenesis of which the successive stages were not fossilised and are missing. According to this theory, living man would be closer to the root-stock of the *hominidae* than *Australopithecus, Pithecanthropus* and Neanderthal man. According to the other hypothesis, neoteny (retention of immature characters) has played a major role in human evolution and living man consequently has many infantile, non-specialised features. This hypothesis can be regarded as the application of Bolk's theory of foetalisation to the data recently obtained on human palaeontology.

In any case, as we see, palaeontology has proved definitively that the theory of evolution also applies to man himself.

CHAPTER EIGHT

Bio-geography and Palaeontology

The geographical distribution of living animals supplies essential arguments in favour of evolution. Darwin himself noted in his *Journal* in 1837 that his observation of Galapagos Islands finches during his voyage of exploration in the *Beagle* was the mainspring of the idea of evolution. The islands of the Galapagos Archipelago—there are thirteen of any importance—are inhabited by a special sub-family of Fringillidae (to which our finches belong)—the Geospizinae. These comprise fourteen species known only in the Galapagos (except for one which can be found further north, in the Cocos Islands). Five species of *Geospiza* live on the ground and feed on seeds. Two others have left the ground and live on cactus. Five more Geospizinae are arboreal and are classified with the genus *Camarhynchus*. One of these species has a pointed beak with which it catches insects in the manner of a woodpecker. Other species (*Gerthidea*) are also insectivorous. The beaks of these different species are quite distinct and related to their diets. Endemism (the relative importance of the original forms) is stronger in the outer islands of the archepelago than in the central Galapagos. These facts can be understood only when one accepts that from a common source these Geospizinae evolved locally in different directions, following different adaptations. These Geospizinae represent a remarkable example of adaptive differentiation.

In other cases biogeography can be understood only in the light of palaeontology. Resemblances between the fauna of two continents which are now separated, for example, may imply that in the course of earth's history these continents were once joined together. The resemblances can be understood only if we accept that a genus (or family, or order) which appeared in a certain part of the world had been disseminated (in accordance with the theory of evolution) from that base.

The concept of evolution does not in fact imply merely that species are transformed in the course of geological time. It also forces us to accept that systematic units or taxons (order, family, genus, species) came into being successively in the course of earth's history. Now when a new taxon appears there is no reason (except in the case of marine organisms) why it should necessarily exist simultaneously everywhere on the surface of the earth or in widely separate regions.

In other words:

1. If the geographical distribution of taxons of terrestrial organisms is now found to be widely disconnected, palaeontology should enable us to show that these taxons had a much more uniform, world-wide distribution in the course of the earth's history.

2. If the fauna of islands or certain parts of the world (for instance South America) is of a certain composition, with many genera and species which can be found only in these areas (extreme endemicity), this means that the areas have been geographically isolated for rather a long time.

3. If organisms adapted to life on land are present in synchronous geological formations in two different areas, this means that these areas have been linked by a continental connection.

The fact that the distribution of terrestrial organisms actually conforms to these rules, which are a result of the very concept of evolution, is an indirect proof of evolution.

I. Scattered Geographical Distribution

1. The example of living dipnoans is classical. This class of fish is represented in modern nature by only three genera: *Neoceratodus* in Australia (this fish lives only in two Queensland rivers), *Protopterus* from Central Africa and the South American *Lepidosiren*. According to the transformists, this distribution can be explained only by common origins. Now these origins are proved by palaeontology: in the Devonian, the dipnoans lived in Europe, Greenland, North America, Siberia and Australia. The ancestors of *Neoceratodus* existed in large numbers in the Triassic but since these fossils are mainly represented by isolated teeth and their skeletons are not generally known, the name *Ceratodus* is preferred, because there may ultimately prove to have been features differing from *Neoceratodus*. *Ceratodus* teeth have been found almost all over the world from the Triassic and Jurassic, but from the end of the Jurassic onwards the area of distribution of the genus *Ceratodus* regresses and contracts. (They were still numerous in the Sahara in the Cretaceous era.) The first *Neoceratodus*—scarcely differing from the living one—appears in the Upper Cretaceous of New South Wales. Fossils related to *Protopterus* and *Lepidosiren* have also been found in the Oligocene of Fayum.

2. The case of the tapirs is to some extent comparable. These ungulates with an odd number of toes (perissodactyls) exist currently in India and South America. It is easy to explain this distribution when we remember that all these species of tapir are descended from a common ancestral form, as palaeontology confirms. The family of the Tapiridae appears in the Oligocene of Europe and the United States with the genus *Protapirus* (which may not be homogenous). The genus *Tapirus* appears in the Miocene and has been found in the fossil state in Europe, North and South America and Asia.

3. Ichthyologists have noted that the fauna of Mediterranean teleosts today is comparable to that of Japan but differs from

those of the Red Sea and the Indian Ocean. Present-day Mediterranean and Japanese fauna originated with an Oligocene Palaeomediterranean fauna, which we know well thanks to the work of C. Arambourg, and which dates from an epoch when the Palaeomediterranean, or Tethys, stretched from the area of the present Alps, which had not yet risen, to Japan. In this example too, the distribution of living organisms can be explained only by palaeontological evolution.

II. The Settlement of Populations in Islands

A. *Madagascar*
Although the Mozambique Channel was temporarily open in the Permian, it was only at the end of the Mesozoic era that the island was finally separated from the continent. It is this separation which enables us to understand why present-day and fossil Malagasy fauna are extremely unique. The Carbon-14 dating recently undertaken on the sub-fossil fauna of Madagascar has in fact shown that this fauna was very recent. In the South-west of the big island, at least, the fauna, had already begun to decline by 2,000 BC and had disappeared as a whole by 1,000 BC.

Grandidier was the first to draw attention to these sub-fossils when he discovered vertebrate bones 35 km north of Tulear in 1866. Then the initiative of a number of researchers, especially Lamberton and the Malagasy Academy, led to the discovery of many deposits, some in caves and others—the most numerous—in marshy depressions.

This native fauna included giant turtles which have now disappeared (*Testudo grandidieri*). There are giant tortoises in the Seychelles as well but not on the African continent. It included a giant bird, *Aepyornis*, which seems to have been known to the natives in the 17th century, a hippopotamus, *Hippopotamus merlei* (there is no longer a hippopotamus in Madagascar) and above all, the Lemurs.

The Lemurs, or Pro-simians, comprise the lemuriforms which are now exclusively Malagasy, and the lorisiforms, which we now see only in Indo-Malaysia and Africa (*Nycticebus* of Bengal, Cochin China and Indonesia, *Loris* of India and

Ceylon, *Galago* of East Africa). One feature which sets these two groups apart is the anatomy of the tympanic region.

The living Madagascar lemuriforms—of which there is no genus elsewhere in the world—belong to two families, the Lemuridae and the Indridae. In general the Lemuridae have a "fox-like" muzzle and separated toes, whereas *Indri* have somewhat rounder heads and their toes are connected by a membrane. The genus *Daubentonia*, with a single pair of hypsodont incisors, cannot be included in these two families. The Lemuridae cover the genera *Lemur, Lepilemur, Hapalemur, Cheirogaleus, Microcebus, Phaner*: the Indridae, *Indri, Avahi* and *Propithecus*. But the sub-fossil Madagascar lemuriforms are also quite numerous: a species of *Daubentonia* larger than the living one has been discovered, lemurs which are sturdier than living forms (*Pachylemur*), a massive form, *Megaladapis*, whose skull alone is 30 cm long and which is reminiscent in some respects of the Suidae (FIG. 72), and the Indridae (*Palaeopropiethecus, Archaeoindris, Mesopropithecus*, etc.). The Archaeolemuridae are particularly interesting, covering the two genera *Archaeolemur* and *Hadropithecus*, of which the outstanding feature is the development of the brain-case and the shortening of the face, a trend running parallel to the one seen in true apes.

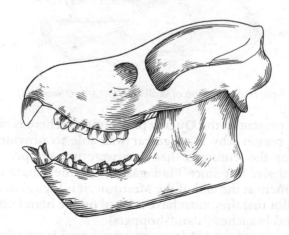

FIG. 71.—*Megaladapis*: reconstruction of skull (× 1/6). (*After Osman Hill*)

The Madagascar lemurs must have been able to evolve and differentiate owing to the rarity of carnivores in Madagascar; of the seven genera of carnivore living in the big island, the best known are Cryptoprocta and the Madagascar genet or fossa. It does look as if these Madagascar lemuriforms are the descendants of the Eocene lemuriforms such as those which we know from the Paris Basin, the Adapidae. (The other hypothesis, which according to J. Piveteau is less probable, would be a relationship between Madagascar lemurs and Adapidae.) The lemuriforms appear in the European Palaeocene (Cerney-les-Reims Thanetian) with the genus *plesiadapis* (FIG. 73) with its big incisors, like *Daubentonia*, but with no more far-reaching affinity with that genus. *Adapis* (FIG. 72), already described by Cuvier in the Montmartre gypsum,

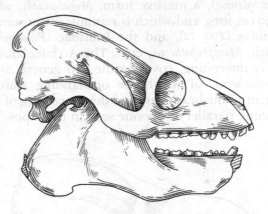

FIG. 72.—*Adapis*: reconstruction of skull (× 2/3). (*After Osman Hill*)

was also present in the Quercy phosphorite. There is no doubt that the reason why Madagascar was able to provide such a refuge for the lemurs is that they were not the prey of carnivores there. But since Madagascar became separated from the continent at the end of the Mesozoic, it is logical to concede with Millot that they must have arrived on the island on rafts of leaves and branches (island-hoppers).

The history of the Madagascar insectivores is parallel to that of the lemurs. Madagascar's living insectivores are Tenrecidae.

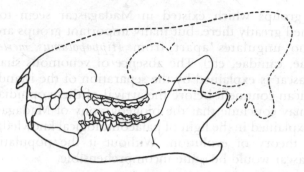

FIG. 73.—*Plesiadapis*: reconstruction of skull (× 1 app.). (*After Matthew and Simpson*)

Covering at least six genera, these are very primitive in certain respects (the crown of their molars is not yet greatly differentiated so that it has a V-shape as in the Zalambdodonts, or something like a W-shape as in the dilambdodonts) and really represent a source-group of insectivores. Anatomically they are related to the genus *Palaeoryctes* (FIG. 74) of the New Mexican Palaeocene. In the same way Cryptoprocta, although a viverrid (the group of civets and genets) has marked similarities to a felid carnivore of the Oligocene, the genus *Nimravus*. It seems

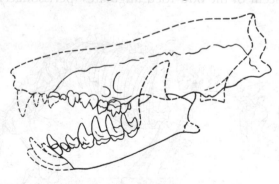

FIG. 74.—*Palaeoryctes*: restoration of skull (× 7/3). (*After Matthew*)

that this genus is close to the common origin of the felids and viverrids. Madagascar also has some endemic rodents (the Mesomyinae family) with dental crowns which converge with those of other, non-Malagasy rodent families.

The groups which existed in Madagascar seem to have flourished greatly there, but many important groups are missing (no ungulates apart from *Hippopotamus merlei*, no hyenidae, canidae, etc). The absence of venomous snakes in Madagascar is explained by the separation of the island from the African continent before the arrival of these ophidians.

We may conclude that the biogeography of Madagascar is easily explained in the light of palaeontological knowledge and of the theory of evolution. Without it the population of Madagascar would be quite incomprehensible.

B. Australia

The outstanding feature of the Australian fauna is the presence of egg-laying mammals, the monotremes, which are unknown elsewhere in the world (*Ornithorhynchus* and *Echidna*) and the preponderance of marsupials. These occupy a variety of ecological niches corresponding to the adaptations of placentals in other areas of the globe. The marsupial carnivore is *Thylacinus*; the phalangers correspond to our squirrels, *Petaurus* to our *Galeopithecus*: *Notoryctus* corresponds to our insectivores, *Phascolarctos* to our lemurs and *Diprotodon* (now extinct) (FIG. 75) is reminiscent of the odd-toed ungulates (perissodactyls).

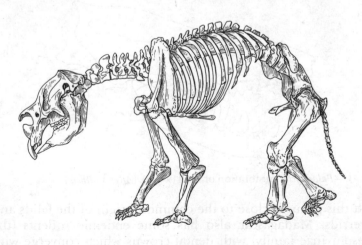

FIG. 75.—Skeleton of *Diprotodon* (× 1/35 app). (*After Gregory*)

However, at present half the genera of Australian mammals are placentals. These have either been recently introduced, like the dingo which was known before the Europeans arrived in Australia and seems to have been a dog descended from domestic dogs introduced by man; or they belong to only two orders, the rodents and the cheiroptera. Marsupial adaptations in Australia are undoubtedly wider than those of the placentals.

The Monotremes have certainly been in Australia for a long time and in view of their primitive features it is probable that they have been living in that country at least since the Jurassic. This hypothesis is also proved by the fact that the living genera, *Echidna* (living in Australia and New Guinea) and *Ornithorhynchus* (known only in Australia) are quite distinct, which suggests a long separation. Almost no Australian fossil Monotreme is known apart from the Miocene genus *Ektopodon* (FIG. 76) defined by molars with crowns divided in two by a

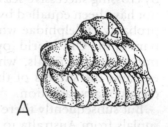

FIG. 76.—Left upper molar of *Ektopodon*: **A,** from the top; **B,** from the back (× 8/3). (*After Sturton*)

deep cross-groove. The genus is now considered to be a *Phalanger* (Marsupial). These molars are comparable to the transitional molars of *Ornithorhynchus* and it seems easy to in-

terpret them from a transformist viewpoint: the dentition of
Ornithorhynchus is the result of a regression from a more advanced dentition.

The demarcation line between Asian and Oceanic mammalian fauna is absolutely clear-cut. It is the Wallace line,
which passes between Borneo and Celebes by way of the
Macassar Straits which lie in an oceanic trough. The large
Asiatic mammalian fauna (rhinoceros, elephant, tiger) live only
to the West of this line and are unknown to the East of it.

The fossil marsupials of Australia are primarily Pleistocene
and Australia's living fauna is less varied than the Quaternary
fauna (genera such as *Diprotodon, Thylacoleo*, etc., having disappeared). A number of Australian marsupials of the Tertiary
era has also been found, from the Oligocene to the Pliocene.
These fossils show that living families were already in existence
in the Miocene, which implies that the island has been occupied for a very long time. The marsupials probably arrived
by crossing successive sea channels, a performance which could
not have been equalled by placentals. These first migrants were
probably Didelphidae which are known from the Lower Tertiary of the Old World (opossum family). The lack of competition from placentals, which are far more recent emigrants,
explains the success of these Australian marsupials and their
evolutionary radiation.

But subsequently there must have been a migration of marsupials from Australia to New Guinea, since the New Guinea
marsupials comprise fewer genera than those of Australia.
Australia and New Guinea have four marsupial genera in common but six genera of marsupials are found in New Guinea
alone, which proves that these animals must have reached the
island quite a long time ago, during the Tertiary, and were thus
able to differentiate.

The only placentals in Australia—apart from the dingo—are
the rodents and the cheiroptera. Rodents are represented by
sub-families and genera peculiar to the island but not by particular families. This situation is explained by the recent im-
migration of these animals which probably began in the
Miocene. Bats, as flying animals, comprise fewer endemic
forms in Australia than do the rodents. These are all forms of

Asiatic origin which came from Asia in successive waves, seemingly from the beginning of the Tertiary onwards.

So we see that the problems posed by Australian biogeography can be satisfactorily resolved by means of evolutionism. The same is true of South American biogeography.

III. Faunal Regions

By way of example we will take a look at the South American faunal region, whose uniqueness has long been recognised. This region, still known as Neogaea, in fact extends beyond South America to the north, covering Central America and tropical Mexico as well.

The living fauna of this region is completely specialised, with marsupials (opossums), edentates (sloths, ant-eaters, armadillos), platyrrhine monkeys, carnivores (jaguars, kinkajous, coatis, [ursidae]), llamas, peccaries, tapirs etc.

From the Palaeocene onwards various large groups of mammals are found in South America. The Palaeocene outcrops are near Rio de Janeiro and in Patagonia. The Palaeocene groups of South American mammals are: (1) marsupials, and (2) placentals. Among these placentals are found Edentata, Condylarthra, Litopterna, Notoungulata, Astrapotheria and Pyrotheria.

The condylarthra comprise archaic mammals of which a typical feature is the pulley-joint of two tarsal bones, the astragalus and the navicular. They seem close to the origins of the ungulates and carnivores.

The litopterna—exclusively fossil and South American—are one or three-toed mammals with molars reminiscent of those of the horse. Some actually resemble closely those of the equids (convergence), but they differ from equids in the serial arrangement of their carpal bones, which alternate in horses. E.g. *Thoatherium* (FIG. 77) and *Macrauchenia*.

The notoungulates, also exclusively fossil, have limbs with the same characteristics as those of the litopterns, but their teeth are similar to rhinoceros' teeth. They appear in the Palaeocene and develop, culminating in the Pleistocene in giant forms such as *Toxodon* (FIG. 78).

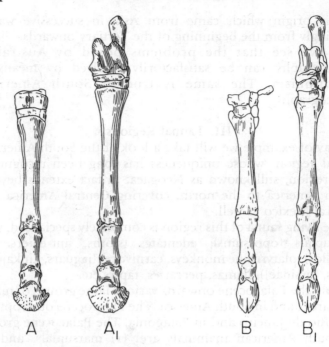

FIG. 77.—Comparison of manus (**A, B**) and pes (**A₁, B₁**) of the horse (**A, A₁**) and *Thoatherium* (**B, B₁**). (*After Gregory*)

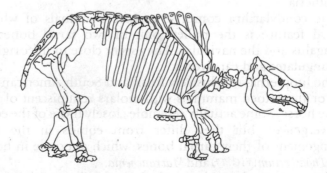

FIG. 78.—Reconstruction of skeleton of *Toxodon* (× 1/30 app). (*After Gregory*)

The astrapotherians—an exclusively South American group—comprise generally rather large ungulates with large, rooted canines developing into tusks. In the main genus,

Astrapotherium (Patagonian Upper Oligocene), the body was about 3 metres long, the face short (FIG. 79), the upper canines very powerful. The cheek teeth were not unlike those of the rhinoceros. Astrapotherians are known from the Palaeocene to the Miocene. These animals seem to have established themselves in proximity to the condylarths.

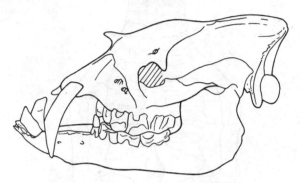

FIG. 79.—Skeleton of head of *Astrapotherium* (× 1/8). (*After Scott*)

To some extent the appearance of the pyrotherians was similar to that of the proboscideans. Like them, they probably had a trunk, the incisors had become tusks and the cheek teeth had two parallel cross-crests each. These pyrotherians (FIG. 80) are known from the Eocene to the Oligocene. Their origins seem to lie with the archaic ungulates which were among the first occupants of the South American continent.

What is the origin of these different groups? Marsupials are known from the United States Upper Cretaceous: they belong to the same group as the opossums. A number of authors have therefore assumed that South American marsupials were of North American origin, but the opposite hypothesis has also been suggested, and since Cretaceous marsupials are rare this is by no means improbable.

It was also long thought that the South American edentates originated with the North American palaeanodonts. These palaeanodonts are mammals with long, narrow-clawed feet and a few peg-shaped teeth. They are not known in the United States until the Palaeocene but then persist into the Miocene.

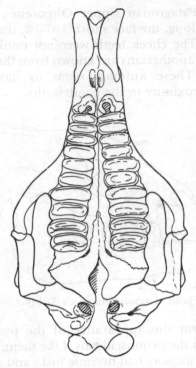

FIG. 80.—Skeleton of head of *Pyrotherium* (× 1/8 app.). (*After Loomis*)

The palaeanodonts seem, however, to be related to the Pholidota (pangolins) and not to the true edentates. It is therefore quite possible that the edentates differentiated locally in South America, starting with mammals of the Upper Cretaceous. The same would be true of the condylarths, litopterns, notoungulates, astrapotheres and pyrotheres. There is, in any case, no clear proof that all these mammals were emigrants coming from the north during the Palaeocene. But whatever the origin of these groups, this and their geographical distribution in South America alone can be explained only by the isolation of that continent at various stages of the history of the earth, and by the evolution of the vertebrates.

The groups of mammals of the South American Palaeocene

went on individualising locally, to reach their apogee either in the Eocene (notoungulates, litopterns, marsupials), or in the Miocene and Pliocene (edentates). South American fossil marsupials are generally carnivores, whereas the Tertiary placentals are herbivores in this part of the world. As they did in Australia, some South American marsupials developed in a direction parallel to that of the placentals: for instance, the genus *Thylacosmilos* (Argentine Pleistocene) (FIG. 81), is a true sabre-tooth tiger comparable to *Smilodon*, but marsupial. There is also the remarkable variety of edentates represented by the armadillos, anteaters, glyptodonts and gravigrades (*Megatherium, Neomylodon, Scelidotherium*); all these genera are, moreover, very recent and became extinct only some ten thousand years ago.

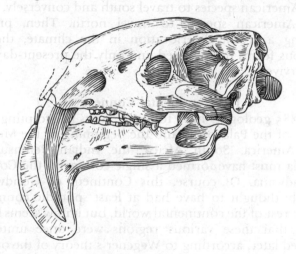

FIG. 81.—Skeleton of head of *Thylacosmilus* (× 1/3 app.). (*After Riggs*)

The Oligocene saw the arrival of fresh immigrants, monkeys and hystricomorphic rodents. They must have reached South America by moving from island to island (island-hoppers) but there is no consensus as to the route they followed, since some authors maintain that their origins were North American, others African.

In the Upper Miocene the procyonids to which the coatis

belong appeared in South America only. They, too, are island-hoppers, probably of North American origin.

In the Pleistocene, on the other hand, immigrants began to arrive in South America not in isolation but in a whole Nordic wave: carnivores, fissipeds, horses, tapirs, peccaries, cervids (deer), camelids, mastodons. During the same period, South American groups reached North America (armadillos, gravigrades, glyptodonts, some porcupines). The migration of the armadillos is in fact still going on across the northern United States. The armadillos have invaded the country by ad-vancing along the railway embankments. The sudden modification of the mammalian fauna of South America im-plies the existence of the Panama Isthmus in the Pleistocene. This may have acted as a filter bridge, enabling only certain North American species to travel south and conversely, certain South American species to travel north. Then, probably following a recent deterioration in the climate, the most numerous forms disappeared and only the present-day fauna have survived.

IV. Continental Connections

Since 1885 geologists have followed Suess in accepting that at the end of the Palaeozoic and the beginning of the Mesozoic, South America, South Africa, the Indian Peninsula and Australia must have formed a single continent, the Continent of Gondwana. Of course, this Continent of Gondwana is generally thought to have had at least sporadic connections with the rest of the continental world, but it now seems beyond dispute that these various regions were once united and separated later, according to Wegener's theory of the origin of continents. But if the Continent of Gondwana did exist it would imply that there were similarities in the composition of the Permo-Triassic vertebrate fauna, for instance those of South Africa and South America. Palaeontologists have now demonstrated that these two faunas are actually related.

There was a small Permian reptile, about 60 cm in length, visibly adapted to aquatic life, although it had well-developed but feeble limbs with which it could walk on the ground; the mouth of this animal, Mesosaurus (FIG. 82), was filled with a very large number of needle-teeth and was a positive fish-trap. Now, this mesosaur is only known in South Africa (Dwyka formation corresponding to our Lower Permian) and Brazil (Itarare formation practically contemporary with Dwyka).

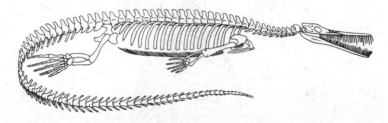

FIG. 82.—Skeleton of *Mesosaurus* (× 1/5 app). (*After McGregor*)

The Lower Triassic is represented in South Africa by strata of the Beaufort formation which is part of the South African continental Permo-Triassic still known as Karroo. These strata are known as the areas of *Lystrosaurus* and *Cynognathus*. The genus *Lystrosaurus* (FIG. 83) is an herbivorous mammalian reptile (dicynodont) while the genus *Cynognathus* (FIG. 84) is a mammalian reptile but a carnivore (theriodont). The Lower Triassic is known in the Argentine in Mendoza Province. In South Africa, in addition to *Lystrosaurus,* there is a very large form of dicynodont, *Kannemeyeria*, and among the theriodonts, in addition to *Cynognathus*, the genus *Diademodon* (FIG. 85), in which the crown of the molars has cusps as in the mammals (gomphodont arrangement). Recently, the Argentine palaeontologist Bonaparte has found *Cynognathus, Kannemeyeria* (FIG. 86) and a gomphodont (*Colbertosaurus*) in South America.

The Gondwanian fauna of the Middle Triassic is in fact known for the number of its gomphodonts and the presence of rhynchocephalians (reptiles still represented today by the one genus *Sphenodon* from New Zealand, with the temporal arch defining the bottom of the lower temporal fossa still complete, in contrast to the present arrangement in living lizards). The Middle Triassic in Africa has produced fossils, in particular in Tanzania (Manda deposits) and the Karroo (Molteno deposits). The Manda deposits contain gomphodonts and there is at least

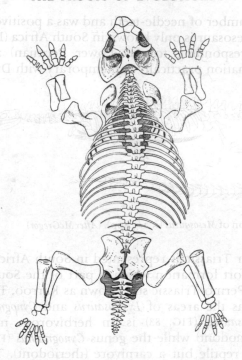

FIG. 83.—Skeleton of *Lystrosaurus* (× 1/7 app.). (*After Broom*)

one gomphodont genus in the Molteno deposit (*Scalenodon*). Similarly, many and varied gomphodonts have been collected in South America (they belong to the family of the traversodonts and come from the Chañares, Ischigualasto (Argentine), and Santa Maria (Brazil) deposits). There is also a rhynchocephalian, *Stenaulorhynchus*, from the Manda deposits, while the Santa Maria and Ischigualasto formations contain another rhynchocephalian, the genus *Scaphonyx*.

These similarities between the fauna of two continents which are separate imply that the two continents were closely linked at one time in the history of the earth. The similarities are understandable only if we accept that a genus (or family or order) which appeared in a particular area of the earth, spread (in accordance with the theory of evolution) outward from that area.

Conversely, palaeontology makes it possible to check the

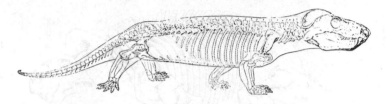

FIG. 84.—Skeleton of *Cynognathus* (× 1/25 app.). (*After Gregory*)

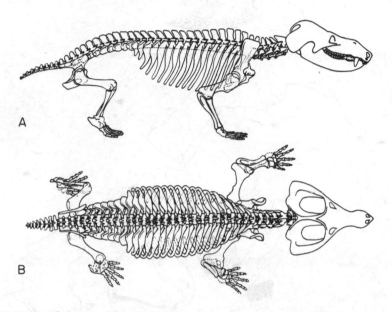

FIG. 85.—Skeleton of *Diademodon* (× 1/10 app). **A,** Lateral view; **B,** Dorsal view. (*After Brink*)

value of palaeo-geographic reconstructions. For instance, it is generally accepted that during the Triassic Madagascar was squeezed between the African coast, India and the Antarctic (FIG. 87) and close to these different areas. So Madagascar must have been in a more northerly position than it is today, with its southern tip touching the coast of Somalia. This hypothesis is not currently confirmed by vertebrate palaeontology, since there is almost no species of stegocephalians and reptiles common to South Africa and Madagascar. This does not mean,

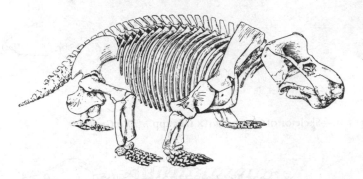

FIG. 86.—Skeleton of *Kannemeyeria* (× 1/25). (*After Pearson*)

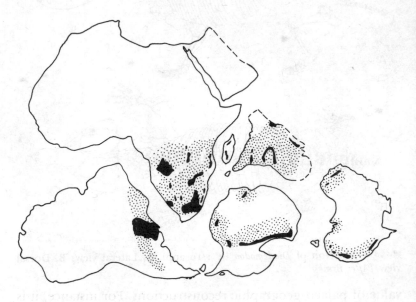

FIG. 87.—Palaeographic reconstruction of the relative positions of Madagascar, Africa and India in the Triassic. (*After King*)

however, that the hypothesis is necessarily false, but that the peculiar nature of the Malagasy fauna has still to be explained.

CHAPTER NINE

Palaeontology and Embryology

The anatomy of living creatures can be explained both as the result of the evolution of species and as the outcome of an individual development in each organism. The various stages of individual development often remind one of ancestral features. The similarities between stages of individual development and extinct species cannot be the result of chance. This "recapitulation" is an indirect proof of animal and vegetable evolution.

For Haeckel, parallelism between the development of individuals and the evolution of species was a positive law to which living beings were subject. "The organic individual repeats in the rapid and brief course of his individual development the main changes of form to which his ancestors have been subjected in the long, slow course of their palaeontological evolution . . . ."

But Haeckel was wrong. In reality, although it is true that certain embryonic arrangements can be understood only as reminders of previous stages of evolution, there are obviously many examples of developments which are not recapitulatory.

We will first consider examples of recapitulation in the course of normal development and then show that in certain results from experimental embryology, archaic anatomical arrangements may occur.

In the course of its development a living crinoid, the comatula (*Antedon*) is fixed during its larval existence—except in the very first stages—on a stalk consisting of a column of superimposed plates. Then the animal's calyx separates at the base from the column, which afterwards disintegrates. Now, fossil crinoids are almost all stalked and the stalk of the developmental stages of the feather-star can therefore be interpreted as a reminder of an ancient organisation, even though we know of many stalked crinoids today which have retained the archaic arrangement.

Similarly, in the course of development of living fish (*Amia* for instance), we observe that the skull is formed by separate longitudinal cartilaginous elements of which the most important, at the level of the floor of the cranium, are the trabeculae in front and the parachordals at the back (on either side of the anterior part of the dorsal midline). This can be seen in the *Amia* for example, a North American fresh water ganoid fish, the embryology of which is particularly well-known. The existence of the trabeculae and parachordals (FIG. 88) actually corresponds, as the American palaeontologist Alfred Romer has pointed out, to the division of the brain-case into two parts, articulated together, in the extinct crossopterygian fish. In both cases, in the embryos of living fish and in the crossopterygians, the separation, either between trabeculae and parachordals or between the two articulated sections of the brain-case, is situated slightly behind the hypophysis. How can this similarity be explained without assuming a relationship—however distant—between the living fish and crossopterygians?

The mode of formation of the fins in the agnatha and fish has been the subject of a good many hypotheses by the anatomists. According to these: 1 The paired fins have developed during the history of life from a paired natatory flap, by a concentration of the internal and external radials of this flap; 2 among the unpaired fins, the caudal, of heterocercal origin, became homocercal in the course of evolution. Various palaeontological data confirm these hypotheses. As far

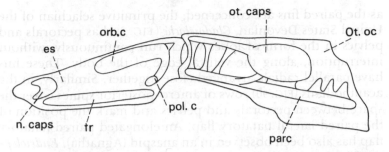

FIG. 88.—Embryological Interpretation of skull of a Rhipidistian Crossopterygian (*After Romer*): **n. caps.**, nasal capsule; **ot. caps.**, otic capsule; **orb. c.**, orbital cartilage; **pol. c.**, polar cartilage; **es**, ethmosphenoid portion of braincase of rhipidistian; **ot. oc.**, otico-occipital portion of rhipidistian braincase; **parc.**, parachordal; **tr.**, trabecula.

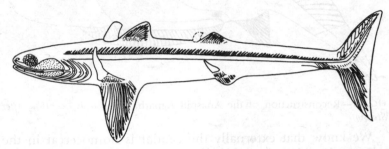

FIG. 89.—Reconstruction of skeleton of *Cladoselache* (× 1/10 app.). (*After Dean*)

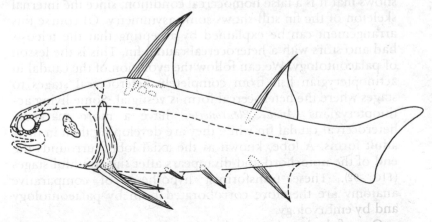

FIG. 90.—Reconstruction of Acanthodian *Diplacanthus* (× 3/4). (*After Watson*)

as the paired fins are concerned, the primitive selachian of the United States Devonian, *Cladoselache* (FIG. 89) has pectorals and pelvics in the form of lobes which run continuously, without interruption, along the ventral edge of the body. These fins have parallel radials arranged close together. Similarly, in the acanthodians (FIG. 90) rows of antero-posterior spines cover the space between pectorals and pelvics and mark the position of the paired lateral natatory flap. An elongated paired natatory flap has also been observed in an anaspid (Agnatha), *Endeiolepsis* of the Canadian Upper Devonian (FIG. 91).

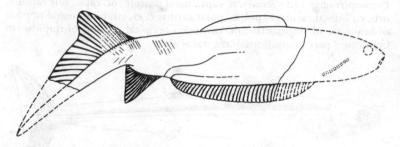

FIG. 91.—Reconstruction of the Anaspid Agnatha *Endeiolepis* (× 5/8). (*After Stensiö*)

We know that externally the caudal is homocercal in the teleosts, but that the internal anatomy of this fin in the fish shows that it is a false homocercal condition, since the internal skeleton of the fin still shows some asymmetry. Of course this arrangement can be explained by accepting that the teleosts had ancestors with a heterocercal caudal fin. This is the lesson of palaeontology. We can follow the evolution of the caudal in actinopterygian fish from completely heterocercal stages to stages where the heterocercal form is vestigial. Some living actinopterygians (*Amia, Pleuronectes*) have a more markedly heterocercal caudal fin while they are developing than in their adult forms. A lobe, known as the axial lobe, surrounds the end of the notochord and disappears after the youthful stages (FIG. 92). These transformist hypotheses of comparative anatomy are therefore corroborated both by palaeontology and by embryology.

One of the best-known theories of comparative anatomy is

that of Reichert (1837). According to this, the otic bones of the middle ear in mammals are homologous: 1 to the hyomandibular in fish (stapes); 2 to the quadrate in reptiles (incus); 3 to the articular in reptiles (malleus); 4 to the angular in reptiles (tympanum). This theory has been verified both by palaeontology and by embryology. During the evolution of

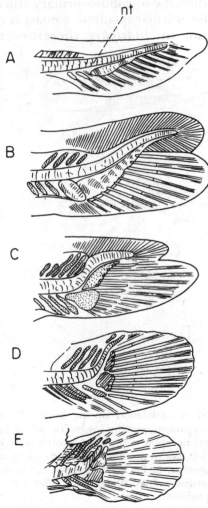

FIG. 92.—Successive stages in the development of the caudal fin of the halibut, showing the transformation which takes place as a heterocercal fin grows into a homocercal one: older and older successive stages from A to E. (*After Goodrich*)

mammalian reptiles, as we have already seen, the bones at the
back of the lower jaw (basically articular and angular), regress
(FIG. 93) at the expense of the dentary, whose surface increases.
In the end these bones are situated in a narrow groove on the
median face of the jaw, the *sulcus cartilaginis meckeli* (see Chapter
Six.). But in the embryos of certain mammals (*Didelphys*, from
La Sarigue), a stage of development has also been observed in
which the squamoso-dentary articulation does not yet exist but
the articular quadrate contact is retained. This special condition in *Didelphys* therefore seems to be basically a

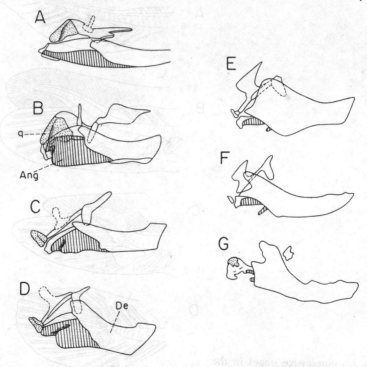

FIG. 93.—Evolution of the lower jaw in the mammalian Reptiles and
comparison with the lower jaw of the Sarigue embryo: A. Lower jaw of
archaic reptile (*Captorhinus*, a cotylosaur); B. Jaw of a pelycosaur (*Dimetrodon*);
C. D. Jaw of primitive therapsids (Gorgonopsians): C, *Leptotrachelus*; D, *Arc-
tognathus*; E. F. Cynodont jaws; E, *Cynognathus*; F, *Protacmon*: G. Jaw of the
Sarigue embryo (Didelphys). (*After Watson*): **Ang**, angular; **De**, dentary; **q**,
quadrate.

recapitulatory feature of the evolutionary history of mammals.

Some embryological experiments do not in fact seem to be explicable other than in the light of the transformist theory.

In living birds the fibula is generally not highly developed by comparison with the tibia, although in some genera the fibula does reach the tarsal bone which follows it distally, the fibulare. In the chicken the fibula is poorly developed and looks like a bony needle ending in a point at the level of the distal third of the tibia. Nevertheless, in this animal the fibula is longer in relation to the tibia and reaches the fibulare in the very first days of incubation. It is only after the fifth day that the growth of the tibia overtakes that of the fibula. Moreover in *Archaeopteryx* the fibula is elongated and welded distally to the fibulare. In the chicken the growth of tibia and fibula compete, but the archaic type of competition—that is the one in which the fibula develops fully—can be restored by various subterfuges (Hampé): 1 if a leaf of mica is inserted in the chicken embryo between the rudimentary fibula and tibia, in its subsequent development the fibula will equal the tibia in length; 2 if, still in the chicken embryo, the end portion of an old bud of the back foot is excised and a whole young back foot bud is grafted onto the excised surface, the result is a normal foot except for a larger fibula (FIG. 94), with the long fibula ending

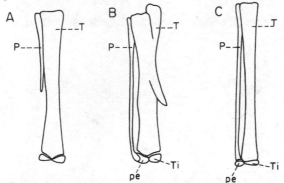

FIG. 94.—Variation in length of the fibula in birds: **A.** In the normal chicken embryo the fibula is more than half the length of the tibia on the tenth day of incubation; **B.** In experiments (see text) the fibula reaches the fibulaire; **C.** The fibula of Archaeopteryx is as fully developed as in case **B. P,** fibula; **Pe,** fibulare; **T,** tibia; **Ti,** tibiale.

either in a point alongside the tibia, or with the fibula over-
taking the tibia distally, or with the lower extremity of the
fibula coming into contact with the fibulare. In other words,
Hampé succeeded in reproducing experimentally in the
chicken a structural *Archaeopteryx* stage of foot. An experiment
like this shows that as far as the back leg of the chicken is concerned, the *Archaeopteryx* stage is obsolete but still latent and
may reappear under certain experimental conditions.

CHAPTER TEN

Palaeontology and Genetics

In previous chapters we have shown how the study of fossils, either by itself or in association with other sciences—biogeography, embryology—has produced many indisputable proofs of the existence of the evolution of species and groups. Does palaeontology enable us to reconstruct, even partially, the genetics of extinct species?

We have not discussed evolutionary theories in this study. Our intention was to convince the reader of the reality of evolution independent of subjective attitude. Now, the theories of evolution are only large hypotheses, attempts at synthesis, trying to reassemble the results acquired from several biological disciplines. Among these hypotheses, neo-Darwinism accepts that evolution is the consequence of natural selection acting on mutations occurring in individual populations of the same species. We shall not attempt to discuss the validity of this theory here but simply note in passing that the name neo-Darwinism is not very logical, since Darwin himself knew nothing of mutations (see Chapter Eleven). If palaeontology could provide proofs in favour of neo-Darwinism this would indirectly demonstrate, since this theory accepts evolution, the merits of transformism. But conversely, if palaeontology does not furnish conclusions as to the validity of neo-Darwinism, this certainly does not imply that evolution does not exist, or that the documents concerning the history of life (that is fossils) are insufficient to substantiate the theory, or that another theory of evolution (e.g. Lamarckism, typostrophism, etc.) is valid.

We know that the neo-Darwinians regard mutations as one of the essential factors in evolution. Can evidence of genetic mutation be found among the palaeontological documents? The initial difficulty is a theoretical one. It is clear that for the geneticists mutation can be mentioned only on condition that we are speaking of pure trends, otherwise the reappearance of a recessive characteristic might be taken for a mutation. Now, it is obvious that palaeontology allows for observations, but not experiment. So one should be able to deduce from the appearance of a characteristic (in the vertebrates, generally associated with a tooth or a bone) that one is dealing with a mutation: for instance, Simpson claimed that when in an individual *Phenacodus* described by Osborn an additional cuspid appeared on the right and left lower second molars, this arrangement represented a mutation. Although we may agree with Simpson that this is the probable interpretation, we certainly cannot regard it as proven.

In the same way, the appearance of the crochet on the crown of the upper molars of *Parahippus* is regarded by Simpson as a mutation. In the equids we give the name crochet (or caballine fold) to a special process of the transverse ridge of ivory surrounded by enamel (metaloph) on the molar crown of these animals. In fact, the Oligocene horses *Mesohippus* and *Miohippus* do not always have crocheted molars, but only sometimes, in a few individuals; this characteristic, which is regarded as mutational, becomes constant when we move on to *Parahippus*. Simpson therefore believed that the fossil *Mesohippus* and *Miohippus* are vestiges of populations in which the characteristic "presence of a crochet" is infrequent and has not yet been segregated. But this is simply one interpretation of the facts.

Moreover, the fossil evidence is almost always incomplete and fossils may also very often change size after the death of the animal (especially shells). Under these conditions, if one can attempt to reconstruct the phylogenesis of these major trends it is clear that it cannot be established as a genealogy. Palaeontology cannot produce evidence of the existence of well-defined genetic mutations in past fauna.

Furthermore, the neo-Darwinians believe that the species is a statistical concept defined not by a precise morphological type but by the variability of cross-fertile populations. So we are asked to represent living and fossil species by curves of histograms expressing the variability of one characteristic of a genetically homogenous population. From the genetic standpoint this process is acceptable because the geneticist is generally interested in the heredity of a small number of characteristics within a species. Such a process would not normally be acceptable for the graphic representation of the characteristics of one species in relation to another, at least if these are defined by sufficiently complete profiles. In this case, in fact, the large number of characteristics involved will enable the species to be defined only in multi-dimensional space, or else the species will have to be represented by a large number of two-dimensional diagrams. Henceforth the comparison between two species, one of which is a descendant of the other, will usually become practically impossible without numerous calculations of correlation coefficients. Such calculations may, however, confirm the validity of the similarities observed between two species without necessarily arriving at definite consanguinities. Under these conditions, a diagram representing the evolution and transformation of two successive species (FIG. 95) seems to us to express only one interpretation.

On the other hand, the fact that the material of palaeontology consists of fossils collected in layers of terrain further complicates the problem. A "population" of fossils with the same appearance and from the same deposit may very well be represented by a bell-curve without that population being genetically homogenous. Some authors have actually considered that a representation of this kind—the consequence of random effects—involves a post-mortem collection of fossils. Instead of describing a population of contemporaneous organisms (biocoenosis) it would merely represent an assembly

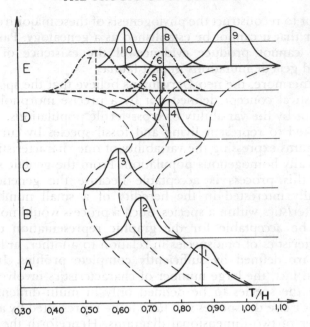

FIG. 95.—Attempt to define different species of Kosmoceras from various geological levels (from A to E) by means of the distribution curves of the relationship T/H (thickness/height of contour). Middle Callovian. (*After Tintant*)

of organisms which had in common the fact that it had died owing to physical factors (thanatocoenosis). We are therefore unable to accept the following postulate on which palaeontological studies have been based: "If we consider a collection of fossils coming from a precisely defined level of a single bed in the same site, we are entitled to claim that this collection represents a fauna made up of practically contemporaneous elements, at least on the scale of geological time, and that it can be considered as an isochronous population." (H. Tintant). The reservation "at least on the scale of geological time" seems in contradiction to the very concept of isochronicity.

We can therefore conclude that the palaeontologist: 1 is usually unable to know if he is dealing with mutations among the fossils he is studying; 2 that because of the time factor his observations almost always apply to biocoenoses fossilised one after another, of which the individuals are probably mixed. Palaeontology does not, therefore, enable us to draw conclusions as to the precise consanguinities of fossil species of animals defined by statistical methods.

This does not mean that the biometry of fossil forms cannot produce interesting results for palaeontology. I simply wanted to offer a reminder that it is difficult to apply the data of population genetics to fossils without a good deal of hypothesis. On the other hand, I am convinced of the necessity of defining the species in palaeontology by as comprehensive a statistical and biometrical study as the material allows, numerical data being, of course, more accurate as a source of information than mere qualitative conditions. However, the fossil species is obviously much less precise than the living species, since the cross-fertility criterion cannot be taken into account and not least because of the rarity of certain fossil items, some palaeontological "species" being defined, in many cases, by a single, incomplete specimen.

CHAPTER ELEVEN

Conclusions

In the preceding pages we have shown that the study of fossils provides the most irrefutable proofs of biological evolution. Its existence is consequently now considered as the basic principle of the history of life which it is the palaeontologist's aim to track down. Unfortunately, the fossil evidence is incomplete and gives us only a partial picture of the evolution of living creatures as it took place. The first organisms, up to the beginning of the Cambrian, have in fact generally been destroyed by metamorphism, a process resulting in the crystallisation of deep sedimentary rocks. Consequently the origin of a large number of invertebrate groups is lost to us. As we have seen elsewhere, the study of fossil vertebrates is the main source of examples in favour of evolution. The result is that the vertebrate palaeontologist is usually essentially a biologist, whereas the invertebrate palaeontologist (apart from the specialists in certain groups such as arthropods, echinoderms, etc.) is usually more of a geologist.

One frequent objection to the validity of palaeontology is that fossils are relatively scarce. Organisms have of course only a small chance of being preserved by fossilisation and palaeontology is therefore able to provide us with only sparse and more or less accidental information—fragmentary information, at the very least. It is of course quite true that fossilisation is an exceptional process especially for the soft forms of life although the same is not true of shelled forms, for instance. We shall never have a complete inventory of the organisms which have existed from the pre-Cambrian onwards. To retrace even the history of the trends is not the basic aim of the palaeontologist, however, who is really trying to find out the major directions of evolution.

Moreover, the destruction of organisms after death should generally balance out statistically within the various groups. But it is obvious that we know the palaeontology of forms with hard portions (shells, bones) better than that of those animal groups which are entirely soft.

The example of vertebrate history certainly shows that there are many problems of evolution still to be solved. For instance, the origin of the reptiles is still unknown. For a long time the reptiles were thought to stem from the stegocephalic seymouriamorphs. The genus *Seymouria* (FIG. 96, 97) is in fact

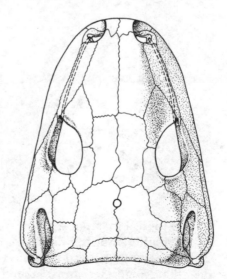

FIG. 96.—Restoration of upper face of skull of *Seymouria* (× 3/5). (*After White*)

very similar to a reptile, the genus *Diadectes* (both *Seymouria* and *Diadectes* (FIG. 98) come from the Texas Permian). It therefore

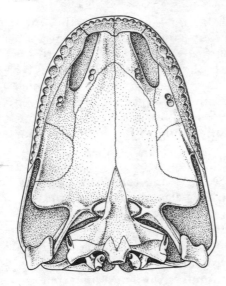

FIG. 97.—Restoration of under-
side of skull of *Seymouria* (× 3/5).
(*After White*)

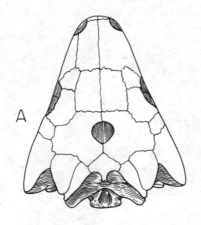

A

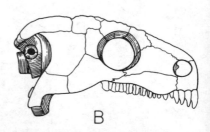

B

FIG. 98.—Restoration of the skull
of *Diadectes* **A** seen from above
and **B** from the side (× 1/3 app).
(*After Watson*)

seemed logical to suppose that *Seymouria* could be the ancestor
of the reptiles. But the discovery of the columella (stapes) of
Diadectes (FIG. 99) proved that this bone had a very special form
and that Diadectes must therefore represent a decadent
branch, without descendants, to which *Seymouria* is related. But
Seymouria has no connection with the other reptiles: it must

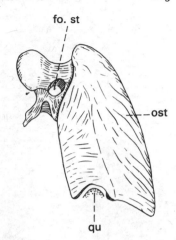

fo. st

—ost

FIG. 99.—The stapes of *Diadectes:* **fo. st,** stapedial foramen; **ost,** ossified part of stapes and tympanic membrane; **qu,** quadrate. (*After Olson*)

qu

already have taken off along a specialised path. The similarity between the hyomandibular of the rhipidistian crossopterygians (such as *Eusthenopteron,* for instance) and the stapes of the pelycosaurian reptiles (we know that the stapes of the reptiles is homologous to the hyomandibular of the fish) has also been used as an argument in favour of the direct descent of the reptiles from the crossopterygians; but there is no known intermediate stage between rhipidistians and reptiles. For the time being, therefore, the origin of the reptiles is one of the enigmas of vertebrate palaeontology.

However, in other respects, the results obtained by the vertebrate palaeontologists have radically altered our conceptions about these animals.

The simplified diagram below (FIG. 100), taken from Stensiö, is a synthesis of modern views on the vertebrates. From an hypothetical primitive stage—the Eocraniates—they separated into two super-classes: one, with the ostracoderms and living cyclostomes, is that of the agnatha; the other that of the gnathostomata. The agnatha, lacking differentiated jaws as their name indicates, cannot be the ancestors of the jawed vertebrates or gnathostomata. The disposition of the branchia (FIG. 101) is in fact radically different in the two groups: in the agnatha the gills are internal in relation to the arch supporting

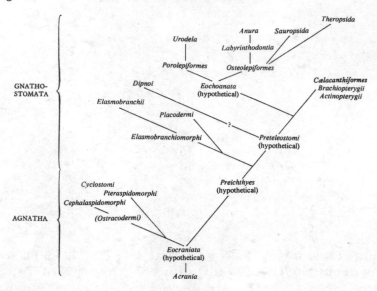

FIG. 100.—Evolution of the Vertebrates. (*Stensiö*)

them and both anterior and posterior half-gills of the same arch carry the same nerve; in the gnathostomata, on the other hand, the gills are external in relation to the arch and the two halves of the gill in one arch carry two different nerves. These two arrangements are incompatible and show that although agnatha and gnathostomata must have had common ancestors but that the gnathostomata cannot be the descendants of the agnatha.

Among the agnatha two main trends can be distinguished:

1 The Cephalaspidomorphi, comprising the Osteostraci, the Anaspidae and the Petromyzontidae (lampreys), the last two orders being the only living ones;

2 the Pteraspidomorphi, with the fossil Heterostraci and the living Myxinoidei.

We do not know the direct ancestors of the fish (Preichthyans)

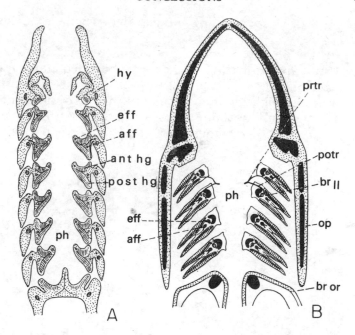

FIG. 101.—Diagrams showing the visceral (branchial) apparatus in the Agnatha (A) (*left*) Agnatha and (B) in Gnathostomata. (*After Jarvik*): **aff.** afferent branchial artery; **hy**, hyoid arch; **br II**, branchial arch II; **eff**, efferent branchial arteryl **ant hg**, anterior half-gill; **post hg**, posterior half-gill; **op**, opercular; **br. or**, branchial orifice; **ph**, pharynx; **potr**, postrematic branch of branchial nerve, **prtr**, pretrematic branch of a branchial nerve.

but the fish—comprising a number of classes—do not represent a systematic unit. One of the first assemblies of fish, the Elasmobranchii, includes the placoderms (armoured fish, with the arthrodira in particular) and the elasmobranchs. Dipnoi form a second class, as do the actinopterygians on the one hand and the coelacanthoforms on the other hand. The appearance of internal nostrils or choanae is the characteristic of the rhipidistian crossopterygians, with their two main orders, the porolepiforms and the osteolepiforms; in all probability the osteolepiforms were the ancestors of the labyrinthodonts (via forms more or less close to *Ichthyostega*, see Chapter Six) which in turn gave birth to the Anura, while the porolepiforms are related to the Urodela (though we do not know of fossil genera filling the gap between these last two orders).

As for the reptiles, they are not homogenous, which is why they do not appear in this list; they are subdivided into at least two main phyla (FIG. 102) the theropsids and the sauropsids (however, although the individuality of the theropsids, which include mammals, is quite certain, the sauropsids do not appear to be homogenous and comprise several distinct trends).

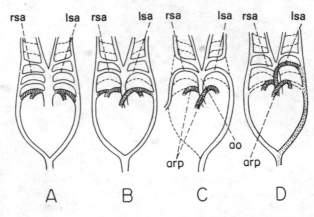

FIG. 102.—Vertebrate circulatory system: **A,** Amphibian; **B,** Hypothetical intermediate stage. **C,** Theropsid; **D,** Sauropsid. **ao,** dorsal aorta, **par,** pulmonary artery; **rsa,** right systemic arch, **lsa,** left systemic arch.

We see that in such a scheme the classes of zoological categories founded by the neontologists have either disappeared or, like birds and mammals, play only a subordinate role. This is because the principles governing these two types of classification are not the same: for palaeontologists the classification has to represent the history of life and trace the major stages of evolution; for zoological neontologists, on the other hand, the classification is a practical one which does not trace true affinities but only similarities observed in the living world. It is said that palaeontological classification is vertical, neontological classification horizontal. Now, from the evolutionary standpoint, only the vertical classification is valid. According to this, the classes of fish, amphibians and reptiles cannot be retained and have to be subdivided. In reality the fish correspond to agnatha and gnathostomata of the following classes: Elasmobranchiomorphs, Dipnoi, Actinopterygians, Coelacanthiforms, Rhipidistians. The Stegocephalii and the Anura stand opposite, among the amphibians, to the Urodela. As to the reptiles, the Theropsida as a whole—including the mammals—stand opposite to various sauropsid lines, which include the birds.

This book has not, moreover, been concerned with theories of evolution. Theories of evolution try to determine the actual *causes* of the transformation of organisms. Since there are a number of hypotheses on this subject, the public sometimes has the impression that the divergence of opinion among the scholars implies some scepticism with regard to the real existence of evolution. In this work we have therefore concentrated on producing the evidence of transformism without examining the validity of the different theories. However, it is obvious that the only valid theories must be those which are not in contradiction to the history of life as it took place and as palaeontology has been able to reconstruct it. Furthermore, since palaeontology represents the actual science of evolution in its concrete reality, this historical discipline is obviously not capable of explaining on its own the biological mechanisms which give rise to the transformation of living creatures.

So what are now the main theories of evolution?

1 Darwinism, in its ancient and classical form, has broken down. In Darwin's day, no one had heard of mutations. According to Darwinian theory, selection would have allowed only those individuals to survive which were the best adapted and which passed on their characteristics to their descendants. Like Lamarckism, this concept therefore assumed that acquired characteristics were hereditary.

Darwinism has little connection with the theory known as neo-Darwinism (still called the "modern" or "synthetic" theory of evolution by its supporters), except that the latter retains the role of natural selection as fundamental, but applies it to populations. Evolution is said to be a "gigantic experiment in population genetics" (L'Héritier). Basically, mutations are said to take into account the formation of new systematic units, whereas natural selection explains adaptation. Moreover there is only one type of evolution, since it was this which resulted in the appearance of new mutations: the appearance of a class, family or order (mega-evolution in Simpson's terminology) is thought to be of the same order as the formation of a genus or species (macro-evolution according to Simpson; micro-evolution concerns mutations). The theory was developed mathematically according to the formulae of population genetics and in particular by defining a coefficient of natural selection, s; this is linked to Δp, frequency variation of a gene from one generation to the next in a population, according to the following ratio:

$$\Delta p = \frac{sp\,(1-p)^2}{1 - sp\,(1-p)^2}$$

where p represents the initial frequency of this gene. This theory was initially developed by geneticists (Tessier, J. Huxley, Wright, Haldane etc.) and was clearly formulated by Simpson, in particular.

2 Lamarckism emphasises the role of the use or non-use of organs. Use strengthens them, non-use results in their atrophy. The transformations acquired during the animal's lifetime become hereditary (as long as they are common to both sexes). Experiment has not confirmed the hypothesis of the heredity of acquired characteristics, but Lamarckism is still defended by many palaeontologists. We have seen above that mutations could not be observed in fossils (see Chapter Ten). On the other hand, the problem of adaptation to the environment is quite obviously fundamental for those palaeontologists who wish to reconstruct the manner of life of extinct animals. The original concept has undergone improvements. Berg, for instance, claims that evolution is the consequence of the action of environmental factors (choronomic factors) according to a Lamarckian mechanism, and of autonomous factors. At the same time, Osborn distinguishes between adaptations by modification of the proportions of organs (known .as alloiometron) resulting from the prolonged action of the en-

vironment, and autonomous adaptations, called aristogenic, which are not perfectible by the action of the environment.

3 Other theories depend entirely on internal factors. They claim that evolution is independent of environmental factors. It is autonomous. It must be understood not as an ectogenesis but as an autogenesis. Evolution is said to consist of a modification of organizational plans brought about by internal factors. According to Schindewolf, for instance, each phylum passes through a rapid stage in which it establishes its organisational plan (or "type" in Schindewolf's terminology): typogenesis. This plan is then stabilised during the typo-stage. Finally, the organisational plan is, as it were, dissolved into various types towards the end of the phylum: typolysis. The overstatements of this theory are obvious (for instance, all phyla clearly do not pass through these three phases); but above all it does not explain adaptation. It seems very probable that internal factors do play a role in evolution, however. Nopsca, for instance, attributed the gigantism of the dinosaurs to hyperpituitarism. On the other hand, there is a relationship between the development of the individual (ontogenesis) and the evolution of the species (phylogenesis), whether the former recapitulates the latter, or, on the contrary, ontogenesis is extremely slow and consequently juvenile characteristics persist in the adult (neoteny). It is rare to see a completely new method of development appearing which seems independent of the parent forms. The relationship between development and evolution implies the existence of the role of internal factors.

4 Certain authors believe that the truth lies in a synthesis of these different concepts. For instance, Goldschmidt explains macro-evolution on the basis of systemic mutations which are related to chromosomic aberrations. Micro-evolution alone is thought to correspond to genetic mutations. According to Heberer, on the other hand, micro-evolution takes place in accordance with a neo-Darwinian model, but the determinism of macro-evolution is more complex. In addition, it should be noted that Berg's and Osborn's theories, quoted under 2 above, are really syntheses of the theories of Lamarck and the autogeneticists 3.

What criticism can be made of these theories from the stand-point of palaeontology alone? Palaeontology teaches us that trends are directed, that evolution often unfolds in parallel within different phyla, that the history of life shows us many examples of convergence.

We have looked at examples of the orientation of trends above. For instance, in the equids the structure of the limb gradually tends towards monodactylism, in the camelids, towards a two-hoofed foot with a cannon-bone. A feature of the human trend is a tendency for the brain to grow in volume. Trends should also be regarded more as complex bushy growths with certain dominant evolutionary tendencies than as simple branches. This orientation of trends is called orthogenesis. Now, on the one hand, authors do not agree even on the meaning of this term; and, on the other hand, they interpret orthogenesis as the result of various causes. For the neo-Darwinians, for instance, orthogenesis is simply orthoselection; it is the result of natural selection acting in the same direction in the course of phylogenesis. Of course, it is possible that this interpretation is valid in some cases, but in various examples it seems to us to be defective. We know that in the actinopterygian fish—bony fish with paired, radiating fins—we observe a straightening of the preopercular. Having first sloped towards the eye, in evolved form this bone straightens and becomes vertical or even backward-sloping. This straightening is seen recurrently: in the Aeduellidae (FIG. 103) from the Permo-Carboniferous, and a different trend in the Haplolepidae, and also in the Parasemionotidae family in the Triassic (FIG. 104). Fish with an evolved cheek therefore

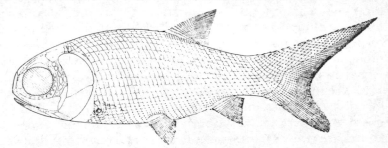

FIG. 103.—Restoration of the body of *Aeduella* (× 2/3 app). (*After Heyler*)

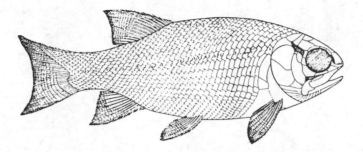

FIG. 104.—Restoration of the body of *Parasemionotus* (× 1/2 app.). (*After Lehman*)

co-existed with fish with an archaic cheek for a period of much more than a hundred million years. It therefore looks as if the arrangement of the cheekbones was irrelevant to natural selection. Similarly, man is characterised by a brain of large volume, with complexes fissures. However, it is not at all evident that the acquisition of a large brain of the modern type was the outcome of natural selection. The brain (FIG. 105) of the giant Brontotheriidae (mammals which disappeared in the Oligocene) is very similar to that of living Rhinocerotidae and yet these Brontotheriidae are extinct. This raises doubts as to the advantage of possessing an evolved encephalon (Mlle Edinger). Therefore, in the case of the evolution of the encephalon, orthogenesis seems to have arisen independently of natural selection. It should be noted that this example does not favour Lamarckism either, but supports only the autogenic theories.

As to parallel evolution, there are many examples of this. We have already discussed the cheek of the actinopterygians and the straightening of the preopercular, which took place in several trends. In the same way, in various mammalian reptiles we can observe the regression of the bones behind the lower jaw, the articular and angular, at the expense of the dentary which, on the contrary, develops both upwards (coronoid apophysis) and backwards.

We also know that there are marsupial families living now which have adapted in parallel to placental families: now, this parallelism is also known in fossil marsupials and placentals.

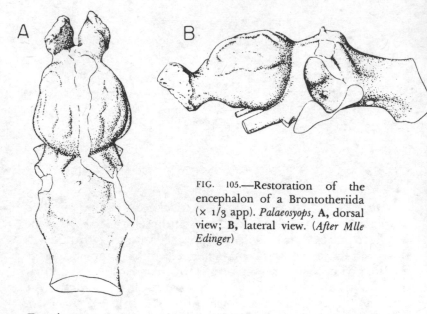

FIG. 105.—Restoration of the encephalon of a Brontotheriida (× 1/3 app). *Palaeosyops,* **A,** dorsal view; **B,** lateral view. (*After Mlle Edinger*)

For instance, the genus *Thylacosmilus* (FIG. 81) of the South American Pliocene displays huge, dagger-shaped canines, like the placental "sabre-toothed tiger" (*Machairodus* and *Smilodon*). ·

The second palate also appears in parallel in different groups. The name "second palate" is given to a partition formed by the median lamellae of the palatine bones and jaw-bones and separating the nasal fossae of the mouth. This arrangement took place independently in at least two lines of mammalian reptiles, the bauriamorphs and the cynodonts. A secondary palate also exists in the crocodiles and marine turtles of to-day (FIG. 106).

It is difficult to explain these examples of parallelism by the action of natural selection alone. The existence of a secondary palate certainly does represent an advantage, but how are we to understand why life has reacted, under very different environmental conditions, (the turtles with a secondary palate are sea-creatures, the mammalian reptiles land animals) with "inventions" of comparable anatomical arrangements?

Sometimes evolution in different trends culminates in related anatomical strutures: this is the phenomenon of con-

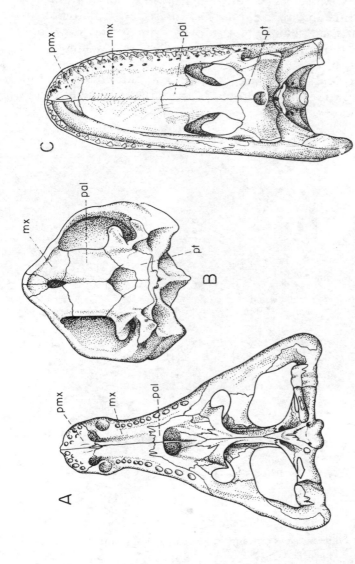

FIG. 106.—Secondary palate: **A**, of a mammalian Reptile (*Cynognathus*); **B**, of an Eocene turtle (*Stereogenys*); **C**, of an Alligator. **mx**, maxillary; **pal**, palatine; **pmx**, premaxillary; **pt**, pterygoid. (*After Romer*)

vergence. Two types of convergence can be distinguished: 1 those linked with adaptation: these are analogies (to anatomists, an analogy is a similarity due to the same function); 2 those which seem independent of any adaptation: homomorphy.

Flight and swimming adaptations culminate in convergences: the wing (FIG. 107), the organ of flight, has a

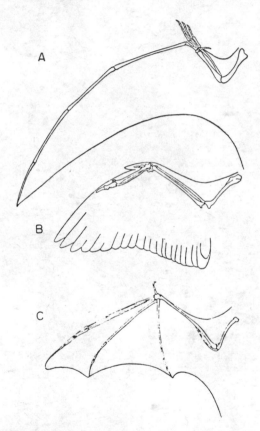

FIG. 107 —Different types of wings in Vertebrates: **A,** Flying Reptile; **B,** Bird; **C.** Bat.

different structure in the flying reptiles (pterosaurs), birds and bats; but in these three examples it is the arrangements which are different. On the other hand, in both pterosaurs and birds, the dorsal vertebrae are fused alongside the scapular girdle in one rigid organ, the notarium (FIG. 108), sometimes regarded as equivalent to a scapular pelvis. This structure is particularly well-developed in *Pteranodon*, a giant flying reptile of the Cretaceous era.

FIG. 108.—Notarium of *Pteranodon*. (*After Eaton*)

Adaptation to swimming, however, is manifested mainly in the shortening of the radius, cubitus and humerus and the acquisition of multiple, often prismatic phalanges, all comparable in form. These conditions can be seen in the cetaceans, ichthyosaurs, plesiosaurs and mosasaurs. The convergence of the ichthyosaurs and dolphins is demonstrated outstandingly in the reduction of the pelvis and absence of a sacrum.

Finally, one other classical example of convergence linked with adaptation is that of the horses and litopterns (see Chapter Eight). In the litoptern *Thoatherium*, of the Patagonian Miocene, the body weight rests on the middle toe of the foot as it does in horses, but the arrangement is less well-adapted than in the horse because the carpal and tarsal bones are arranged in series, contrary to those of the equids (FIG. 77), and not alternating.

These examples of adaptational convergences can be interpreted more easily from the Lamarckian than from the neo-Darwinian standpoint. When distinct lines of evolution culminate in very comparable adaptations, it would imply that natural selection has acted in exactly the same way in these varied examples. This seems inexplicable.

On the other hand, homomorphisms seem to favour the autogenic theory: here are some examples. In the Dipnoi the

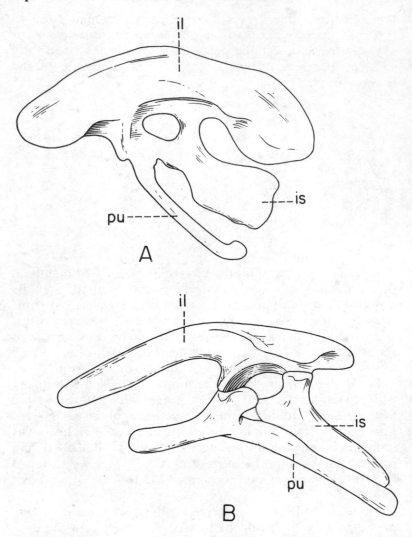

FIG. 109.—Comparison of pelvis of a bird and an avipelvian: **A,** Pelvis of 7-day chick (*After Abel*); **B,** Stegosaurus (*After Marsh*): **il,** ilium, **is,** ischium; **pu,** pubis.

palato-quadrate is welded to the cranium as it is in the tetrapod vertebrates, yet these animals are not descended from the Dipnoi. At the same time the Dipnoi, like the tetrapods, have well-developed cerebral hemispheres (from the Devonian forms onwards). The placodonts, though they differ greatly from the turtles, also have a body enclosed in armour. The classical example of this is the convergence of the avipelvian dinosaurs and the birds. In both groups: 1 the pelvis has four branches (tetraradial pelvis) (FIG. 109); 2 the bones generally have thin walls; 3 the front limbs are generally reduced in comparison to the back limbs; 4 the external digit of the foot often points backwards or is missing. Again, the appearance of the crowns of the tritylodont post-canine teeth is convergent with that of the molars of multi-tubercular mammals.

It is quite obvious that these ideas of parallel evolution and convergence overlap. So the last stages of convergent trends also represent parallel evolutions. Nevertheless it is sometimes difficult to distinguish analogous convergences from homomorphism.

I hope that the above has shown how the orientation of trends, parallel evolution and convergences were generally difficult to interpret in the light of the various existing theories of evolution. It seems to me that only co-ordinated, directional and to some extent autonomous transformations can take parallel evolution into account. They are still unknown, but their existence can be deduced from palaeontology itself. This is not a philosophical hypothesis. These transformations appear to be logically necessary as the direct consequence of palaeontological observation. We do not know if such transformations can be regarded as genetic mutations. The fact that in living nature they do not seem to be orientated may be the result, among other things, of the stability of the material studied: insects do not seem to be evolving any more in our contemporary world. In any case, any valid theory of evolution must be able to face the test of confrontation with the history of life as reconstructed by palaeontology.

Bibliography

Andrews (H. N.) (1961), *Studies in Paleobotany*, New York & London, J. Wiley and Sons.

Arambourg (C.), Chavaillon (J.) and Coppens (Y.) (1967), Premiers résultats de la nouvelle mission de l'Omo, acad. Sc., sér. D. Vol. 265, no 25.

—, Chavaillon (J.) and Coppens (Y.) (1968), Résultats de la nouvelle mission de l'Omo, deuxième campagne 1968, *C. R. Acad. Sc.*, sér. D, Vol. 268, no. 5.

Auboin (J.), Brousse (R.) and Lehman (J.-P.) (1968), *Précis de géologie,* vol. II, Dunod.

Augusta (J.) (1959), *Les animaux préhistoriques,* Paris, La Farandole.

Axelrod (D. I.) (1959), Evolution of the Psilophyte palaeoflora, *Evolution,* vol. 13.

Banks (H. P.) (1968), *The early history of land plants. Evolution and Environment,* Yale University Press, Edited by Ellen T. Drake.

Bishop (W. W.) and Chapman (G. R.) (1970), Early pliocene sediments and fossils from the Northern Kenya Rift Valley, *Nature.* vol. 226, no. 5249.

—, Chapman (G. R.), Hill (A.), Miller (J. A.) (1971), Succession of Cenozoic Vertebrate Assemblages from Northern Kenya, Rift Valley, *Nature,* vol. 233, no. 5319.

Boureau (E.) (1964–1970), *Traité de paléobotanique,* Masson.

Colbert (E.) (1955), *Evolution of the Vertebrates,* Wiley.

Coppens (Y.) (1970*a*), Localisation dans le temps et dans l'espace des restes d'Hominidés des formations plio-pléistocènes de l'Omo (Ethiopie), *C. R. Acad. Sc.,* ser, D, vol. 271, no 22.

—, (1970*b*), Les restes d'Hominidés des séries inférieures et moyennes des formations plio-villafranchiennes de l'Omo en Ethiopie, *Cr. R. Acad. Sc.*, ser D, vol. 271, no 25.

—, (1970c), Résultats de la nouvelle mission de l'Omo (3 campagne 1969), *Cr. R. Acad. Sc.*, ser. D, vol. 270, no. 7.

Compton (A. W.) (1958), The cranial morphology of a new genus and species of ictidosaurian, *Proc. Zool. Soc.*, London, vol. 140.

Crompton (A. W.) (1963), On the lower jaw of *Diarthrognathus* and the origin of the mammalian jaw, *Proc. Zool. Soc.*, London, vol. 140.

— (1964), A preliminary description of a new Mammal from the Upper Triassic of South Africa, *Proc. Zool. Soc.*, London, vol. 142.

Darlington (P. J.) (1957), Zoogeography. The geographical distribution of animals, *Museum of Comb. Zoology*, Harvard University.

De Beer (Sir G.) (1954), *Archaeopteryx lithographica. A study based upon the British Museum specimen*, Br. Mus. (Nat. Hist.).

Dechaseaux (C.) (1962), *Cerveaux d'animaux disparus. Essais de paléoneurologie*, Masson.

De Lumley (H.) and de Lumley (M. A.) (1971), Découverte de restes humains anténéanderthaliens datés du début du Riss à La Caune de l'Arago (Tautavel, Pyrénées-Orientales), *C. R. Acad. Sc.*, ser. D, Vol. 272, no 13.

Dujarric de La Rivière (R.) (1969), *Cuvier, sa vie, son aure. Pages choisies*, Les Maitres de la Biologie, Paris, Peyronet.

Easton (W. H.) (1960). *Invertebrate Paleontology*, New York, Harper Brothers.

Edinger (T.) (1948), Evolution of horse brain, *Mem. Geol. Soc. America*, Mem. 25.

Emberger (L.) (1968), *Les Plantes fossiles*, Paris, Masson

Fenton (C. L.) and Fenton (M. A.) (1958), *The fossil book*, New York, Doubleday.

Genet-Varcin (E.) (1969), *A la recherche du Primate ancêtre de l'Homme*, Paris, Boubée.

Glaessner (M. F.) (1961), Precambrian animals, *Scientific American*, vol. 204, no 3.

— (1962), Precambrian fossils, *Biol. Reviews*, vol. 37.

Goodrich (E. S.) (1958), *Studies on the structure and development of Vertebrates*, London, Constable and Co.

Gregory (W. K.) (1957), *Evolution emerging*, New York, Macmillan Co.

Hampé (A.) (1960), La variabilité du développement du péroné chez les Oiseaux actuels et fossils, *Bull, Serv. Carte Géol. Alsace-Lorraine*, t. 13 fasc. 1.

Heller (F.) (1959), Ein dritter Archaeopteryx-Fund aus den Solnhofener Plattenkalken von Langenaltheim, *Erlanger geol. Abhand*, vol. 31.

Hill (O.) (1960), *Primates*, Edinburgh University Press.

Hoffstetter (R.) (1970), Radiation initiale des Mammifères placentaires et biogéographie, *C. R. Acad. Sc.*, Paris, t. 270.

Hopson (J. A.) and Crompton (A. W.) (1969), Origin of *Mammals. Evolutionary Biology*, vol. 3, New York, Appleton-Century Crofts.

Jarvik (E.) (1959), *Théories de l'évolution des Vertébrés*. (trad. J.-P. Lehman), Masson.

Kermack (D. M.), Kermack (K. A.) and Mussett (F.) (1956), New Mesozoic Mammalia from South Wales, *Proc. Geol. Soc.*, vol. 1553.
—, Kermack (K. A.) and Mussett (F.) (1968), The welsh Pantothere *Kuhneotherium praecursoris, Journ. Linn. Soc. (Zool.)*, vol. 47.
Leakey (R. E. F.) (1970), Fauna and artefacts from a new pleistocene locality near Lake Rudolf in Kenya, *Nature*, vol. 226, no. 5242.
— (1971), Further evidence of lower pleistocene Hominids from Lake Rudolf, North Kenya, *Nature*, vol. 231, no 5300.
Lehman (J.-P.) (1959a), *L'évolution des Vertébrés inférieurs*, Paris, Dunod.
— (1959b), A propos de la loi de récapitulation, *Bull. Soc. Géol. Fr.*, sec. 7, vol. 1.
— (1962), Paléontologie et théories modernes de l'évolution, *Année biolog.*, vol. 1, fasc. 7–8.
— (1967), Quelques réflexions à propos de l'évolution, *Année biol.*, 4 série, t. 6, fasc. 9–10.
— (1969), Les êtres vivants (l'origine de la vie; l'origine des Vertébrés; les Choanichthyens et l'origine dds Vertébrés Tétrapodes; l'origine des Reptiles; l'origine des Mammifères; les Primates fossiles), *Encyclopédie française; cahiers d'actualité et de synthèse*, contribution á une mise á jour du t. V.
— (1972), *La paléontologie des Vertébrés inférieurs*, La Pléiade, Zoologie III, Métazoaires III, N. R. F.
Müller (A. H.) (1957), *Lehrbuch der Paläozoologie*, Jéna, Gustav Fischer.
Orlov (I.) (1959–1964), *Les Fondements de la paléontologie*, Moscow, Acad. Sc. U.R.S.S. (in Russian).
Osborn (H. F.) (1936–1942), *Proboscidea. A monograph of the discovery, evolution and extinction of the Mastodonts and Elephants of the world*: vol. I (1936), *Moeritherioidea, Deinotherioidea, Mastodontoidea*; vol. II (1942), *Stegodontoidea, Elephantoidea*, New York.
Ostrom (J. H.) (1970), *Archaeopteryx*: notice on a new specimen, *Science*, vol. 170.
Piveteau (J.) (1937), Un Amphibien du Trias inférieur. Essai sur l'origine et l'évolution des Amphibiens Anoures, *Ann. de Paléontologie*, vol. 26.
Piveteau (J.) (1950–1969), *Traité de paléontologie*: vol. I, *Introduction. Généralités, Protistes, Spongiaires, Coelentérés, Bryozoaires*; vol. II, *Brachiopodes, Chétognathes, Annélides, Géphyriens, Mollusques*; vol. III, *Onychophores, Arthropodes, Echinodermes, Stomocordés*; vol. IV, *Agnathes, Actinoptérygiens, Crossoptérygiens, Dipneustes*; vol. V, *Amphibiens, Reptiles, Oiseaux*; vol. VI A et B, *Mammifères*; vol. VII, *Primates, Homme*, Masson.
— (1951), *Images des mondes disparus*, Masson.
Remane (A.) (1956), *Die Grundlagen des natürlichen Systems der vergleichender Anatomie und die Phylogenetik*, Leipzig, Akad. Verlagsgesell.
Rigney (A. S.) (1963), A specimen of *Morganucodon* from Yunnan, *Nature* (London), vol. 197.
Romer (A. S.) (1966), *Vertebrate Paleontology*, Univ. of Chicago Press.
— (1969), Cynodont Reptile with incipient mammalian jaw articulation, *Science*, vol. 166.
—(1970), *Tetrapod Vertebrate and Gondwanaland. Second I.U.G.S. Symposium on*

the Stratigraphy and Palaeontology of the Gondwana System, Capetown and Johannesburg.

Schindewolf (O. H.) (1950), *Grundfragen der Palontologie*, Stuttgart, Schweizerbartsche.

— (1956), *Über Präkambrische Fossilien. Geotektonisches Symposium zu Ehren von Hans Stille*, Stuttgart.

Scott (W. H.) (1937), *A history of land Mammals in the Western hemisphere*, New York, Macmillan.

Shrock (R. S.) et Twenhofel (W. H.) (1953), *Principles of Invertebrate Paleontology*, new York-London, McGraw Hill.

Simpson (G. G.) (1951), *Horses*, Oxford Univr. Press.

— (1965), *The Geography of Evolution*, New York, Chilton Books.

Sloan (R. E.) and Van Valen (L.) (1965a), The earliest Primates, *Science*, vol. 150, no 3696.

— and Van Valen (L.) (1965b), Cretaceous Mammals from Montana, *Science*, vol. 148, no 3667.

Sonneville-Bordes (D. de) (1967), *La préhistoire moderne*, Périgueux, Faulac.

Stirton (R. A.), Tedford (R. H.), Woodborne (M. O.) (1967), A new Tertiary formation and fauna from the Tirasi Desert, South Australia, *Rec. South Australian Museum*, vol. 15, no. 3.

Tintant (H.) (1966), *La notion d'espèce en paléontologie*. vol. 1.

Index

Illustrations are indicated by an asterisk (*). The letter-by-letter system of alphabetization has been adopted.
Compilers: R and R Haig-Brown of Sherborne, Dorset.